True Crime -
Gary Ridgway
The Green River Killer

The Story of America's Most Vicious Serial Killer

James Richmond

Table of Contents

Introduction

South of Seattle, the Green River flows. The blue-gray waters start their path on Mt. Rainer in a small spring and make their winding way through the city of Kent until merging into the Puget Sound, an inlet of the Pacific Ocean. Small creeks feed the waters along the way, building their strength. Hundreds of years ago, the river was used by pioneers as a thoroughfare. For anglers, the water's ample supply draws them to the riverbanks. Locals jump in during the hot summer months to swim or raft down. And until the 1960s, the blood and animal remains from the local slaughterhouse were dumped into the water, washing away into the Harbor. The red bled into the gray-brown water that hardly reflected the green color of its name.

But these animal remains were not the only death to kiss the cold river's water.

People drowning in the Green River was not unheard of, but rarely were bodies found in the Kent County city limits. Most were discovered far upstream in the gorge area. While the river was primarily used in the

1980s for fishing, others discovered it could serve a far more disturbing purpose—to dispose of bodies.

It was a hot summer afternoon, July 15, 1982. The sunlight peeked through the canopies of the thick forest leaves overhead and speckled onto the popular trails.

Two boys peddled their bikes alongside the river. The fresh country air rushed over them. School was out for the summertime, and days like today were spent enjoying the outdoors. But when they rode across Peck Bridge, they stopped. There, snagged on rocks, twisting in the middle of the water's current was a young woman's body. No clothes covered her pale skin aside from a pair of blue jeans tied tightly around her neck, shifting with the water. Her arms and legs were bound with rope.

Horrified, the two boys rode off and contacted the police.

Police and investigators arrived to retrieve the naked body. The only identification they could find were the five tattoos on her skin. Unlike so many other bodies pulled from the cold water, it was clear this young woman had not drowned. Someone had strangled her. With only the five tattoos as a lead for her identity, they put their descriptions in the newspaper.

A local tattoo artist recognized their work and called in.

The body belonged to Wendy Coffield. "I think she lives in Puyallup with her mother," the artist informed them. "She's only sixteen."

Like so many others, the bright-eyed, pretty blonde had come from a complicated and troubled background.

Her single mother struggled to make ends meet for the two of them. Wendy dropped out of junior high and began running away. Once, she returned home to her mother, upset after a man had raped her in his car.

She had been out hitchhiking. Her mother warned her that was what happened when you went off alone. Still, the incident had done little to deter the sixteen-year-old. She continued to offer sex in exchange for cash, walking along the Strip late at night.

It was the fate so many sex workers and hitchhikers faced. From the moment they closed the stranger's car door, they were at a stranger's mercy.

After stealing food stamps, the young Wendy was tossed into prison and then into a foster home. And on July 8, 1982, she never returned after being granted a pass to visit her grandfather. When Wendy vanished, no one started to look for her. They assumed she was just another runaway.

But she had run straight into Gary Ridgway. A man dangerous enough to have a body count, which some believe surpasses eighty murders.

The autopsy proved Wendy Coffield died by strangulation. She had a fractured hyoid bone and significant hemorrhaging in her neck muscles. Her left upper arm bone had been broken. And in March of 2003, minuscule paint drops on the jeans used to choke her were matched by a private forensic laboratory to DuPont Imron paint. It was the same paint used at the Kenworth truck plant, where Gary Ridgway worked in 1982.

But it would take twenty years before investigators would make the official link between Coffield and Ridgway. That summer of 1982, the dreaded killer had begun his reign of terror.

Through August 11, 1982, and March 21, 1983, forty bodies were discovered in the Seattle area. Five of which were pulled from the clear, cool waters of the Green River in the summer of '82.

Behind a pair of thick glasses, the average-looking man with muddy brown hair and narrow eyes fell through the net of suspects. He had been brought in and interviewed for picking up sex workers after one woman reported he choked her. He'd pass a polygraph test and escape the police, get married, and surprisingly move on from his nightmarish acts before cuffs were placed upon his wrists. Gary Ridgway would leave the police frustrated and horrified for years as they desperately searched for the Green River Killer. There was little reason to suspect him.

Throughout his life, Gary was viewed by many as dull and dimwitted. He was unassuming and cruised along the known Strip in SeaTac, eyes scanning for his next victim without raising a note of concern. A road that runs eight miles long, lined with bars, motels, and strip clubs, Gary was a frequent visitor, and there was never a shortage of women. Even with Seattle's rainy weather kicked in, the sex workers gathered underneath bus stops and outside convenience stores, waiting to turn a few tricks. Due to the airport's close proximity, the Strip was home to many abandoned lots and houses where the sex workers brought their clients. In the morning, used condoms and needles littered the roadside.

When Gary drove his truck to the side of the road and spoke to the young women, there was no reason to worry. Gary's non-threatening appearance and demeanor were unalarming. He'd even pull out a photo of his young son to put their worries at ease or walk them through the child's room of his home. Disarmed and relaxed, Gary would strangle them to death. Afterward, he'd look at the dead woman before him, and he'd think, "You made me do it, you bitch, you whore, you worthless piece of garbage." In just two years, Ridgway became one of America's most prolific serial killers, leaving a trail of bodies for detectives to follow. With forty-nine confirmed kills, it is believed Gary killed upwards of ninety.

Gary knew the police wouldn't be searching too hard for the lost women. He was manipulative and careful with each move. He told investigators, "My plan was I wanted to kill as many women I thought were prostitutes as I possibly could. I picked prostitutes as my victims because I hate most prostitutes, and I did not want to pay them for sex. I also picked prostitutes for victims because they were easy to pick up without being noticed."

Like many other killers, Gary developed ritualistic habits and returned to the same dumpsites. At least eight different locations became home to Gary's victims, which he moved to continually elude the police's investigation, covering their bodies in dirt and brush, draped beside logs. He returned to have sex with the corpses and relive the moments of their murders; in his mind, they became his own. When the body began to decompose and he could no longer have sex with them, Gary would ride out searching for his next victim.

Born in a seemingly average family, Gary struggled with school and self-image, mainly when it came to relationships with women. He developed a perverse and twisted relationship with his domineering mother. This relationship bred hatred for women, and Gary felt destined to prove his power and worth.

He handled his killing as though it was his career, taking scrupulous detail in the act as well as hiding the evidence. No trophies were kept. His fingerprints were concealed in gloves, only selecting women who were alone. If they scratched or tore at his skin, he was sure to clip their fingertips.

His acts terrorized Seattle and led to one of the largest and longest investigations in United States history. When asked where he thought he ranked among serial killers, Gary said, "Well, according to the number, probably one of the best, yes."

Crybaby

He was twelve years old when his mother ripped him from his bed late at night and paraded him through the house, embarrassing the child in front of his older and younger brother. Her voice was loud as she shouted, yanking him straight into the bathroom. The water that filled the bathtub was ice cold. She stripped him down with a hurl of insults, belittling her son as he was then thrown into the frigid bath. The water splashed out of the tub onto them both.

But she didn't flinch. This was a repeated punishment—discipline to force the twelve-year-old once and for all to stop his bedwetting habit.

Gary Ridgway, however, would not stop, not for several years.

Mary Rita furiously scrubbed her son's genitals. Oftentimes, she hand-washed him, focusing on his privates while barely dressed herself.

The shame and anger twisted inside of the young Gary as he sat with goosebumps rising over his skin and the cold water hitting him over and over. He hated his mother deeply. Loathed her. The one aching wish to hurt her stirred deeply within Gary and rose to the surface.

It would eventually escape.

Mary Rita Steinman was a beautiful woman. She grew up in Bremerton, WA, and was a high school cheerleader, popular, and intelligent. Growing up, her father was a staunch and strict devout Roman Catholic. When he saw that his daughter painted her fingernails, he brought out a hammer and smashed her painted nails. He believed it was inappropriate for a woman to have such color on their hands.

But the conservative nature of her father did not stop her from going out and finding love.

While the music played around the room at a local USO dance, she could not help but fall for Thomas Newton Ridgway, who was five years older. They were married in 1947. However, few in the Steinman family understood her relationship with Thomas Newton Ridgway. In their minds, the once already married Tom Ridgway was rough and crude—a poor match for the stunning and proper Mary Rita. Worst of all, he was not Catholic. A problem that would continually eat away at their relationship.

Shortly after their wedding, they had their first son, Gregory, and the young couple moved to Preston, Idaho. The beginning was a struggle as they tried to get their feet on the ground. Thomas worked as a driver for long-haul trucks and on construction jobs in the summer months. The income was meager, and early on in the family, it was instilled that nothing was to go to waste. The lack of financial stability and grueling jobs forced Thomas to work for extended periods away from home, often leaving Mary Rita alone with the expanding family.

On February 18, 1949, she gave birth to their second son, whom they named Gary Leon. She had just turned twenty-one. And two years later,

Thomas Edward, known as Eddie, was born. With three growing boys, Tom and Mary Rita had to work harder.

"Dad's income was not fixed," Gregory later explained. "It was easier for them to go and live with other people. Mom used to talk about when they first got married, all they had was a can of soup to split. Lots of times when we were growing up, we had the rice and beans diet."

The couple opened a bar together, but Tom grew tired of men hitting on his wife. Mary Rita was a glamorous woman. She took her time to apply a full face of makeup, wearing her hair in large bouncy curls and wearing tight-fitting jeans, dressing up for every occasion. But owning a bar had too many temptations, and since neither Mary Rita nor Tom drank or smoked, they got out of the restaurant business.

To make ends meet, they grew their own food, and nothing was thrown out. It wasn't uncommon for Tom and the kids to search junkyards for scrap parts. He'd later turn around to sell or use them, a habit that Gary carried on through the rest of his life. A relative described how "He [Tom] often found things, took them home, cleaned them up, and resold them. He used to talk about different places where he'd found the 'treasures.' It was a family trait."

Toward the end of the 50s, Tom returned to working construction and driving. His hours were late and, once again, he'd be gone for days at a time.

Once while he was away driving, baby Eddie became terribly ill. Left with no money for a doctor, Mary Rita resorted to carrying her youngest out in the winter air and laying him down into a cold snowbank. She waited beside her infant son, hoping the freezing snow would lower his temperature. Later, the family believed the high fever left Eddie with lasting brain damage.

It was around the age of five or six, Gary had his first experience with death. He and his brothers each got their own baby duck. But Eddie liked to carry the ducks by wrapping his hands around their neck and ended up killing each one.

While living in Portecolla around the second grade, Gary stood out in the garage, playing with matches. He managed to start a fire. Terrified of what he'd done, Gary sprinted into the house and hid in the basement. He heard the loud sirens of the fire trucks pulling up. He couldn't remember if he received a spanking or not.

Around 1959, Mary Rita called her sister. She'd had enough and planned on leaving Tom but needed help moving the kids and herself back to Bremerton. She packed up their bags and, with the children, returned to her hometown. Shortly after leaving, the issues between the couple resolved, and Tom reunited with his wife and children in Bremerton. They settled in the upstairs of Mary's parents' hardware store. Gary described his grandfather as, "Pretty hard. That's what I got from my mom when she talked about him. He kind of favored my brother over me. He cared more for his store, though." But the cracks in the seemingly happy all-American family were forming.

During this time, Thomas Ridgway landed a job driving tour buses for Grayline; then, he moved up to work at the Seattle-area transit agency Metro. Mary even started a part-time job at JCPenney as a saleswoman.

With these new jobs, the family finally had financial stability, and in the early 1960s, they purchased their first home in Seattle: a rambler in SeaTac at 4404 S. 175th St. Gary was eleven years old. It was a large lot, ideal for three boys to run around and spend hours outdoors. The three Ridgway boys piled together in bunk beds, ran around with the other neighborhood children, jumped in piles of leaves, raced around on scooters, and played games of football and baseball. "We literally crawled on our hands and knees over the area around SeaTac where this [series of killings] was supposed to have happened," Greg recalled. The thick forest beside their home was grounds for exploration and discovery, and the three hiked out to see what they could find. All the while, Gary subconsciously mapped out the land, learned the perfect hiding spots. These were places he would return to with girlfriends and his son to have picnics. It was how he memorized the terrain to one day commit unspeakable acts.

When Tom was home, he and his three boys spent a lot of time puttering around the garage, standing on the cold concrete and tinkering on the car. They considered themselves "Chrysler men." The three boys begged their father to join them in their forest adventures. When he obliged, they packed for a little trip and set out on the trails they knew so well. Thomas would cook up breakfast over the crackles and smoke of an open fire in the morning sun.

After Tom took a second job at a mortuary, he told Gary stories about a coworker who engaged in acts of necrophilia with female corpses. He went into detail about the grotesque act as his impressionable young son listened to each word. These ideas became a focus of Gary's sexual fantasies. "Having sex with someone that is dead because you wouldn't get caught. No feelings. She wouldn't feel it," he'd later explain.

Tom was also open about his hate toward prostitutes and sex workers, finding the likes of them to be awful. A wave of anger and attitude Gary eagerly adopted.

But even with financial stability and a lovely home, issues still brewed beneath the Ridgway's roof. While Gary saw his father as a meek and sniveling man, his mother was the definition of aggressive.

Mary Rita, a devout Catholic, was determined to raise her sons in the faith. Problems arose as Tom Ridgway was not Catholic and was forbidden from the church due to his previous marriage. After being convinced to join, Tom attended all the classes, but the priest forbade his entry because of the divorce. Faith became a severe point of contention in the family. But with or without her husband, Mary Rita dragged her three sons to church every Sunday devoutly until her father passed away.

She was a strong woman, strict with the boys and her husband. Mary Rita wasn't afraid to speak her mind and run the household, keeping it clean and orderly. She expected her sons to do the same. She and her husband fought incessantly. And when they weren't arguing with each other, much of their anger was directed at the three boys. "I could sit up in my treehouse and look in their yard," Bruce Revard, a neighbor and childhood friend, said in an interview. "All I'd hear were cries of 'No, Dad, no,' as they were getting beaten with a belt or a stick or whatever."

When the boys would come home from school, even a slice of bread was forbidden as an afternoon snack. They were not allowed to have any extra food until their supper. When they and their friends became hungry, they opened the pantry hoping to find something to sneak into, but even a can of vegetables would result in severe punishment.

Out of the three boys, Gary seemed to be the primary target for their parents' anger and punishment.

While Greg was intelligent and handsome, taking after his mother, Gary struggled to do well academically. He tested to have an I.Q. of 82, and dyslexia kept him from performing well in the classroom. "It was hard for me," Gary recalled, "I was always being compared to Greg." And though Eddie struggled as well, "Mom pitied him, more than anything else." She felt guilt for the brain damage he suffered as a baby and made excuses for Eddie. In Mary Rita's mind, Gary had no reason to fall behind. He should act more like Greg, and she was sure to let him know her disappointment.

"He didn't necessarily talk a lot. He had trouble reading when he was younger. I don't think he felt he could keep up with the other kids." Greg noticed how the other kids teased his little brother in school for being "stupid." Crybaby, they called him, but Gary suffered from chronic allergies. His eyes swelled, and he could do nothing to stop the tears from running down his face.

By the time Gary entered high school, "I only had one A in high school. I didn't read very well, especially at first. Later on, I wore glasses. There was the combination of kids knocking you and teasing you for wearing glasses and not keeping up with the class on certain things." He was held back, and his grades continued to suffer.

His behavior greatly upset Mary Rita. It seemed, no matter what Gary did, he was unable to please his mother. She began shouting and fighting with Tom about their son. Gary listened, dreading his mother's words. The anger twisted within him, retching violent thoughts. "They were gonna put me in a, a, a special school. I didn't want that. My dad and my mom were arguing about it all the time—and it was uh, for retarded people, and I didn't, wasn't retarded, I don't think, so I was mad at them for wanting to put me away from other kids. And wanting to hurt her or . . . and uh, my uh, hurt her bad."

Still close to the age of fifteen, Gary would wake up in the middle of the night to discover he'd wet the bed. Even in his teenage years, Mary Rita pulled him from bed and threw him in the ice-cold bathwater. It happened at least three times a week, sometimes almost every single night. She'd continue to wash him with her hands, touching his adolescent body.

"Only babies wet the bed," Mary Rita said bitterly. "Aren't you ever going to grow up?"

Gary sat in the cold water, depressed and humiliated as his mother continued degrading him. When the bath time was finished, she'd dry him off even though, at times, he'd become erect from her attention.

A mix of hormones and anger twisted in Gary. He developed some sexual attraction to his mother, describing, "she was a, a female, the opposite sex, and, and a, a woman that I'd like to of, um, been my f— first uh, sex partner. Um, somebody that uh, that was a, a, an ideal body and, and uh, right, the right padding and the right um, uh . . . physical characters of a . . . of a woman that'd be ideal to have sex with. Um, and I think it's almost about all, I think." When Mary Rita would sunbathe, Gary would try to sneak a look or peek down her robe to catch a glimpse of her nipples. Fantasies played in his head, ones that mixed death and pain with sex and lust.

She spoke to her son about how much she enjoyed measuring men who needed to be fit for trousers at JCPenney, how some of the customers would get erections from her physical touch, or the different scents she'd detected when kneeling in front of them.

His hate for her wasn't rooted in her sexuality. He loathed being pushed around by women as his mother did to him. And dark thoughts illuminated in his mind. He thought about stabbing Mary Rita and killing her because of the way she berated him—made him depressed and embarrassed. He longed to hurt her, and that rage came out in other forms. "I thought a—about hurting her, uh, so she'd shut up and uh, leave me alone."

He played with the fantasy of murdering his mother to make her stop. He thought out the different ways he'd inflict torment upon her. "I thought about stabbing her in the chest or in the heart maybe, uh … um … maybe, uh … cut her face and chest." He'd use his hands to choke her to death. He had the desire of "sewing up her vagina."

But he knew it was a dark, demented dream he'd conjured up. Gary had to find other outlets.

He threw rocks at windows, watching the glass shatter. He partook in small-scale arson, dreaming of setting his house on fire while Mary Rita was inside. Gary desired to destroy and take possession of the living through harm. Armed with a BB gun, Gary Ridgway shot and killed many birds. He once took the family cat and locked it inside a heavy ice chest but was sure to hide the cooler somewhere where no one in the family could hear the cat's cries. When he opened the chest, the cat was dead.

In fact, Gary's child behavior is indicative of the three traits defined by the MacDonald Triad. In 1963, forensic psychiatrist J. M. MacDonald put forth the notion that bedwetting, arson, and animal cruelty, were indicative of violent behavior, particularly in serial offenses. Gary suffered all three as a child and teen. Finding a criminal with all three issues was extremely rare.

But they were only the beginning for Gary.

As a teenager, he paid his cousin one penny to see what her vagina looked like. "And of course, I got caught and got whipped, you know."

He began to obsessively consume whatever he could about true crime and the stories of dangerous, evil men.

But these problems manifested unnoticed.

His sexual desire intensified. He wanted more. In Junior high, he began what he referred to as "patrolling" to follow girl classmates home in a state of arousal. "I'd have a … a hard-on and … think of the woman as a goal and be on the opposite side of the street. And find out where she lived." From a distance, he'd lurk behind her, flirting with the fantasy of having her for himself. In the morning, he'd rush to the girl's home and watch.

"But that's what I took my ag—gression on. I couldn't take it out on my mom. I had to take it out on my animals and . . . and the kids . . ."

One afternoon, near a wooded area beside the high school, a first grader played outside. The six-year-old was dressed as a cowboy with a little cowboy hat, boots, two six-shooter guns, and a toy rifle. Sixteen-year-old Gary Ridgway saw the child, and evil rose within him. He approached the boy. "You know, there's uh, there's people around here that like to kill little boys like you," he said. Then he asked the six-year-old if he wanted to head into the woods and build a fort together. The little boy agreed, and he marched into the forest with his cowboy boots on directly behind Gary. They stopped now alone with no one to see. When the boy reached down to pick up a stick, Gary revealed the knife he'd hidden and stabbed the child, cutting through the rib and straight into his liver.

"Why are you killing me?" the little boy asked in panic and fear, watching as the red blood pooled out of the wound and ran down, filling his boots. The front of his shirt was soaked with blood and with each heartbeat more pumped out. A dark laugh erupted from Gary's throat, standing with the knife in his hand, watching with a gleeful grin. He raised the blade, and the petrified boy hoped he wouldn't be stabbed again. Gary wiped the blood from the blade onto the little boy's shoulder, then folded it up. "I always wanted to feel what it would be like to kill somebody."

But as Gary walked away from the grassy knoll, delighted with his act laughing hysterically loud, he was unaware that the young boy ran out of the woods to his home. Blood profusely gushed out of him, but he was taken to a hospital where he stayed for several weeks.

The boy's assailant was never found nor identified.

But the six-year-old was not the last attempt made by Gary as a teenager. During his interview, he told the police what he believed was his first murder, but he was unsure if it was a hallucination. "I don't remember, um, if I did this, or if it's like I said, a dream."

While he and a boy swam in a lake near Seattle, Gary wrapped his legs under the boy's neck and dragged the small child beneath the water's surface. The boy squirmed and fought, but Gary held him until the boy became still and drowned beneath the depths of the cold dark water. When it was over, he pulled the body beneath a dock and left it there. Public records reveal two boys drowned in that lake the year of 1964.

In the Navy

Around the age of fifteen or sixteen, he began to expose himself to a neighborhood girl regularly. She ignored his behavior, Gary said. When they sat on the couch near one another, watching cartoons, Gary unzipped his pants and revealed his penis. It went on for about three or four months. Late one night, Gary snuck to her house and tapped her window, hoping she might come out and have sex with him. Alerted by the sound, the girl called for her father. When the father asked Gary about his midnight appearance, he denied ever showing up and claimed it had been someone else.

It was after another recent rejection, Gary arrived at his old elementary school. In a fit of rage, he broke up to twenty windows, smashing the glass. The police arrested him, and his parents paid the damages. His teenage rampages weren't deterred. He broke into at least two houses and contemplated stealing a motorcycle. He began to drink alcohol excessively and, in a blind drunken state, drove the car into a ditch.

He continued pursuing sexual relations.

Gary Ridgway picked up a young woman from the Seattle Center, offering to give her a ride home. He pulled the car over on the side of the road, overwhelmed with sexual impulses that he had little control over as a teenager. Gary began to force himself on her, wanting to have sex and fondling her breasts. But she refused his advances, and he stopped himself, letting her leave his car.

While attending Tyee High School, Gary's social life began to improve slightly. To the others, he came across as a personable, nice guy. He played freshman football and went to youth group Saturday nights at a local Methodist church. None of the other classmates could guess what dark desires lay hidden beneath his average exterior. "You'd see him going to the principal's office, but nothing bad," a classmate said. A boy, once incessantly teased, had become someone who never really stood out. Even his football coach had a hard time remembering who Gary was. "The picture I keep getting in my mind is of a somewhat smallish kid—5 feet 7 or 5 feet 8, 145 pounds, with wispy hair. Nondescript."

All the while, he continued to struggle with his strained relationship with his mother. He wasn't good enough at home, and at school, he was barely more than a nobody. He told one girlfriend that Mary and Tom had adopted him.

Of course, one young woman noticed him.

The pretty and thin Claudia Kraig began to date Gary sophomore year of high school after they met each other while both working at a supermarket in Burien. It was a relationship Gary would later romanticize. His first real love would end in his first real heartbreak. On the weekends, Gary stopped by Claudia's house to pick her up and drive around for a bit. Sometimes they'd go to the movies; other times, they'd head to the park. Outside under the blue sky, they'd have sex or in the car at Seward Park and a road off Military Road South. There the cover of the tall, thick forests kept away prying eyes. He knew the best spots to take his girl.

These were the hills and trails he paraded through as a child, but Claudia was only the first of many he brought, though she'd leave breathing.

After being held back twice, he was twenty years old when he finally graduated high school and decided to join the Navy. He enlisted on August 18, 1969.

When Gary first left, he was assigned to work as a deckhand on the USS Vancouver. The distance didn't stop his relationship. Claudia and Gary continued to pen one another letters.

Aboard the USS Vancouver, Gary was stationed at Subic Bay in the Philippines. His days were eight hours, constructed of daily assigned duties that included maintaining the ship and caring for equipment. When his job was finished, the rest of his day was free for him and his fellow crewmates to do as they pleased.

Back on land, Gary arrived with the other crewmates to let loose. The naval base was surrounded by bars and brothels. Music played, and the beer was cheap. Often, he wouldn't return to the ship until five in the morning. He stayed away from drugs, only trying marijuana once. For Gary had discovered other vices, which he greatly indulged in. Those nights, it wasn't hard for the young sailor to find extra company. Many local women hung around the bar, most of them prostitutes drawn to the allure of American dollars. Drunk, Gary watched the women dance and walk over to him. They'd sit on his lap and touch him. The fantasies to hurt the Philippine sex workers hadn't started, but other dark ideas formed. "And then I . . . and over in the Philippines I was always having women with . . . walkin' over with a beer bottle in their vaginas, bringing it over to sailors all the time. They'd do it," Gary later described. It was the start of one of his disturbing fantasies, to insert objects into women's vaginas. He would later attempt to stick a beer bottle into one of his sleeping wives after a night of heavy drinking.

While in the Navy, Gary was eager to indulge and paid for the services of sex workers many nights. During his many interviews, Gary admitted that in 1969 something happened with him in the Philippines. "I never got it out of my system," he later said. "I probably should have had counseling . . . I said to Marcia [his second wife] that it probably would have helped me more than anyone else. The $5,500 would have been worth it." He never revealed what occurred, but he fantasized about it for years.

Upon returning, the high school sweethearts tied the knot. Claudia was nineteen years old. During the ceremony, Gary stood proudly in his uniform, and afterward, the two drove out to San Diego to start their new life together.

They found a small apartment near Gary's base. In the beginning, he enjoyed his time with Claudia. "I liked married life. Somebody to come home to and security—somebody to talk to. Security—someone my age— to talk to. Lots of times, you can't just talk to a guy. Regular sex." Claudia told detectives Gary demanded sex multiple times throughout the day.

But the newlywed bliss came to an end when Gary returned to the Navy after six months, leaving his wife alone. She moved out of their apartment and in with another woman who had a boyfriend to save money.

Some of the days away while sailing were full of stress and fear. Gary was placed on a supply ship that moved between the Philippines and Vietnam. He and his other crewmates patrolled rivers on alert, waiting for someone to pop out and shoot at them. But the worst fate he encountered was being bit by a rat. Most of his time was spent hanging aboard the ship, waiting in the hot, humid air.

There was a lot of free time to be had. And Gary took advantage of it.

During the twenty-three months and twenty-eight days spent in the Navy, Gary contracted gonorrhea twice from hiring prostitutes. He would later tell his second wife about his extreme hate for Filipino prostitutes.

After being dishonorably discharged, he returned to San Diego. The return home wasn't a happy reunion. He discovered that Claudia had begun to see a mutual friend of theirs and was in a serious relationship with him.

The two separated, and he began his work at a Kenworth plant, painting cars after moving back to Seattle. It was steady work that varied little.

Part of him hoped Claudia might find her way back to him. But after spending a week in Seattle with Gary to try and salvage their marriage at his parents' home, she purchased a ticket back to San Diego in August. Gary was horrified. "Panic set in. I thought about calling the airline to report a bomb threat." But nothing was done, and Claudia's flight was never stopped. He was left in a whirl of depression and hurt. When he discovered she'd begun dating a black man, he started to tell people she was a "whore." Losing Claudia only added to the humiliation Gary believed women put upon him. His mother and now his first wife, who was his high school sweetheart, had humiliated him. In his mind, they'd all taken advantage of him and needed to pay.

They divorced in 1971, only after a little over a year of marriage.

"OK. What caused you to want to hurt the prostitutes in the first place?" forensic psychiatrist Dr. Robert Wheeler asked Gary.

"Because women hurt me and I was just . . ."

"What woman hurt you?"

"Claudia did. Marcia did."

Happily Never After

In 1972, Marcia Winslow was cruising the Renton loop when suddenly a car pulled up behind her. She stopped, unsure of the vehicle in her rearview mirror. From out of the car stepped a young man with a clean-cut appearance and military manners; she thought it might have been an officer here to write her a ticket.

He introduced himself as Gary Ridgway, and while he wasn't a police officer, he was charming enough and expressed interest in Marcia.

The stunt worked, and the two began to date.

But when they first became intimate, Claudia's name came out of Gary's mouth in the heat of the moment. They moved past the slight mistake, and they moved in together. They were married in 1973; Marcia was close to eighty pounds overweight. Gary believed smaller framed women were unobtainable to him. "The women I tend to love are heavyset people," he later described. "Claudia was pretty slim but . . . the only thing I could pick up was a heavyset woman. My dad would say, 'There's a lot of love in those hills.' That's why I paid to have the [thinner] women love me. Even just being in the car with them. I couldn't pick one up naturally. That was one of the reasons I went out with them. I've got something penned up inside."

In the beginning, the couple moved several times and enjoyed one another. Marcia was a great cook and spent time in the kitchen making delicious meals. He brought her to his favorite outdoor areas for camping and hiking as well as to have sex. Between the thick trees and back roads of Maple Valley, Enumclaw, and North Bend underneath the shade of a canopy of leaves, they'd have sex in many of the same places that Gary would eventually leave behind bodies. His sexual appetite bordered on the extreme. He demanded more from his wife and liked to incorporate bondage. During these hikes in the woods, Gary would suddenly disappear. He'd sneak off, slinking through the forest, practicing being silent. And after Marcia waited and grew increasingly worried, Gary jumped out from the thick bushes, eager to terrify his wife. It was a sinister joke with far more horrifying implications.

He worked his way up to become an established employee at Kenworth's Seattle plant. Dressed typically in jeans and a western-styled button-down, he handled the meticulous job with excellence. Painting trucks took a steady hand and a sharp eye for detail. Gary took his time during those shifts laying down paint, ensuring the left and right sides were perfect matches. During his break, he'd pull out his brown paper bag full of food inside the lunchroom, reading over copies of the Little Nickel, a free classified ads newspaper. When Gary spotted a bargain, he pulled out a little notebook and jotted down the details. Just like his father, he loved to find treasures and scraps to resell.

Though he was seen mainly by his coworkers as friendly and personable, there were several occasions he approached the female employees and began to massage their shoulders, whether they wanted the attention or not. They'd shrug him away, thinking of it as nothing more than Gary being a bit overt with his friendliness.

In 1975, Marcia gave birth to their son Matthew, and the family settled on a home in Fort Way. Following the birth of his son, Gary joined several churches, including a Pentecostal one. Marcia described later how her husband had become almost "fanatical" about religion. He read the Bible throughout the house and while at work. He walked door to door through the neighborhood, attempting to convert his neighbors, but he became furious each time a door was shut in his face. Marcia looked to see tears falling from Gary's eyes during church service, and late at night, he'd watch tv while clutching his Bible.

A rift slowly formed in their marriage.

Marcia strongly felt that Mary Rita wore the pants in the family and dominated their life. Gary's mother had access to his bank accounts, and she made her opinions known. Weekends were spent with his parents, instead of with his wife. One night Marcia recalled that a fight broke out between Tom and Mary Rita. Mary Rita became so enraged she stood up, walked over to her husband, and smashed a plate over his head. Without saying a word, Tom left the room with no retaliation.

When Gary's work switched him to night shifts and Marcia began taking classes during the day, there was less time for one another; their relationship began to dissolve. It only worsened after Marcia had gastric bypass surgery to staple her stomach.

The weight began to fall from her figure, and she began to receive extra attention from other men. Marcia started singing at bars with her newfound confidence and would come home late at night, around 3 a.m. It upset Gary, and his self-consciousness increased. He accused her of sleeping with other men at the motels at Pacific Highway South. Marcia told police the accusation was untrue.

Perhaps at some point in their relationship, the frustration like it had with his mother eventually slipped out. A late evening beneath the night sky, Gary pulled up into their driveway, and Marcia got out of the car, making her way to the front door. They'd been arguing. The two had been drinking at a party. Sheer horror and panic overcame her when a pair of hands wrapped tightly around her neck. She could hardly breathe as the hands twisted tighter. She screamed in terror, fighting back at her attacker.

The hands let go. Air returned to Marcia's lungs as she realized it was her husband who had snuck up behind her, choking her. The skin on her neck throbbed with pain, and Gary scurried to the other side of the car. He dodged around, and when he emerged, he tried to convince her someone else had choked her. Marcia was left stunned with black and blue bruises on her neck.

"The choking of Marcia was one of the major things," Gary revealed. "That turned me on." Choking his wife created the want for more. "Well, after that, I wanted to have sex with a prostitute and kill her doing that."

While Gary accused his wife of sleeping around, he was projecting his faults upon her. After the Philippines, he'd never stopped hiring sex workers.

He had told investigators it was "very possible" he had killed several women during the 1970s, though his memories were unclear. He was never able to recall his first kill, honestly. One incident with a prostitute while living in Maple Valley with Marcia, he could only remember that "some'n went wrong, uh, with the date and I, I killed her."

At night, he came home later and later. He'd often return wet and covered in dirt, offering no explanation to his wife on where he'd been except for his car had broken down. According to Marcia, he had no close friends at the time. No one she would have known her husband to have been with. But she did take note of the Visqueen rolls, protective plastic covering, that he kept in the bed of his truck. Several of Gary's victims would later be discovered covered in Visqueen.

"Why don't you go out and have breakfast by yourself?" Marcia suggested one morning in July 1980. Gary found the request a bit odd, but he wandered out into the woods behind his home. When he returned, a moving van was parked in the driveway. Marcia had had enough, and she was moving out, hoping to have left before he returned.

On July 21, Marcia filed for divorce, including a restraining order. She worried about Gary's temper. In August, Gary also had a restraining order placed against her. Both feared the other would turn violent.

"Having Marcia divorce him was the last thing that Gary wanted," his brother Greg described in an interview. "He wanted to be a father. She used Matthew as a lever against Gary. She'd make him pay child support and then not let him see the kid. Gary paid a lot—$350 a month." He visited with Matthew on the alternating weekends, but the end of their relationship was another slight made by a woman. The child support upset him. He felt like his finances were being bled out, and his anger grew. "It was terrible for me," he later described in an interview. "Missed the boy . . . She moved into an apartment in Kent. Several times, I'd go over there, and I didn't want to harass her . . . I'd just go over and sit in the car a ways away. Didn't have the nerve to go and talk to her. Probably for a month, I'd go over three hours a night. I didn't want to pressure her . . . I wanted to be close to her. Kind of hard to explain to my parents . . . It was hard to tell anybody." They attempted to reconcile, but it only lasted a month. She left a second time, so Gary sold the house. He wanted her back, but Marcia was finished with Gary, and the rejection ate away at him.

The idea of killing Marcia danced in his head. He didn't want others to view him as a "loser" with two failed marriages. He claimed she was partly to blame for his murders. "If I would have killed her, then it's possible that it might have changed my life. I'd only have one instead of 50-plus." He'd been through a divorce once before, and it cost him a fortune. But he knew killing Marcia would put him at the top of the suspect list, so he spared her life, taking out his rage and aggression on the young women he picked up along the way. "I was just so mad at Marcia. She treated me bad during the divorce. I just wanted to kill her."

In mid-July, Gary picked up the telephone and called Marcia. He began to harass her about divorce papers and threatened to get a gun with the sole purpose of blowing her boyfriend's head off. She immediately filed a complaint with the Kentwood Police Department.

In 1980, Gary would be arrested for the first time. While out cruising, he hired a prostitute. During sex, his arms wrapped around her and began choking her, similar to how he choked Marcia. The woman reported him to the police, but Gary simply told them it was an act of self-defense upon being questioned. She'd bitten him. The charge was dropped, and not another question asked.

Now single once again, Gary joined the Parents Without Partners group and met several women. He began dating his first girlfriend in May of 1981. Things moved fast, and Ridgway moved into her West Seattle home. She was unaware of who her new boyfriend was and what he was capable of as he lived within her walls. She consented to allow him to tie her up during sex or visit one of his favorite outdoor locations. But Gary constantly demanded sex from her, and the relationship was becoming solely physical. According to the court records, she noticed how Gary had no other friends and was dominated by women.

She broke up with him and asked him to move out.

He purchased a home on 21859 32nd Street in SeaTac, only a few blocks away from the Pacific Highway South. The house was in a private neighborhood, the kind where neighbors didn't bother each other and didn't pry into one another's business. It was a perfect location for Gary to be left alone and not be asked too many questions. It was 1,150 square feet with three bedrooms and one bathroom. And though Gary's neighbors valued their privacy, they noticed how closed up his home really was. "If I was walking by, I'd say, 'Hi,'" local Debbie Roselieb recalled. "He would just ignore me and walk past. It was more private than rude. It was like he just wanted to be left alone."

December 24, 1981, on a cold winter evening at the White Shutters Inn, Gary went to a Parents Without Partners event. He was with his second girlfriend, whom he met through the group. Though he never took her to his favorite outdoor spots to have sex, at one point during that night, as she told the police, he came to her distraught, claiming he nearly killed a woman. She believed he was referring to a prostitute.

In less than a month, Ridgway met another woman while attending a Parents Without Partners dance. His second girlfriend after Marcia ended their relationship when she discovered he was cheating on her.

February 1982, Gary came home. He looked at his third girlfriend and told her that he had done something. She wanted to know more, but that was all the information he gave her. Ridgway hauntingly told her to pay attention to the news because she might hear something. He would later claim that may have been the day of his first kill. "The only thing I can remember is, uh, killing her at . . . my house, and putting some, putting some uh, putting her clothes on, I'm quite sure, with a, a uh, jeans and a shirt with a, a blouse with white buttons." After he murdered her, he'd drop her body off at Highway 18. Her identity and name were never to be known.

With having to pay the child support for his son Matthew, Gary fell on financially challenging times. He rented out his home to Rose Hahn and her husband while he lived in his garage. He spent time with his girlfriend at her home on the weekend, but other nights were spent elsewhere.

One night in April of 1982, Gary Ridgway drove with one clear goal. He wanted to pay for sex. Daily on his commute, Gary passed the Strip, where he picked up women to murder. That night, Gary was arrested for soliciting a decoy; it was a sting operation.

Two weeks would pass, and he'd be arrested a second time for soliciting by another King County Sheriff.

His girlfriend at the time knew about his arrests, but Gary had explained to her that prostitutes were nothing more than "things" to him. The word things created the idea; he didn't care, but his girlfriend didn't understand that, to Gary, his victims were his possessions—his property. Their relationship would last for the next two years, all the while she was completely unaware of what he did to his "things."

The House off Federal Way

"Well, there were other things going on at that house . . . drugs, stolen property, bikers, and ladies . . . you know, prostitutes, coming over," Gary said in an interview with his defense attorney Mark Prothero. "I never did any of that stuff there. But they were drinking and drugging and partying all the time." During the spring and summer of 1982, Gary did several auto paint jobs on the side at a house located off Federal Way. The home was an active party spot. Bikers came over, and prostitutes hung out as well. Every once in a while, one of the bikers would head to a bedroom and have sex with a prostitute. He claimed in an interview the home belonged to a man named R. J. Wilson.

During the wild parties, where they fell into a drunken stupor, sometimes the men would head off to an abandoned barn and have sex with prostitutes. While in the act, R. J. would snap photos or record videos.

On July 8, 1982, Gary Ridgway encountered Wendy Coffield, and he planned to kill her. He'd been worked up that day and was pissed about his wallet being recently stolen. "Eighty bucks," Gary said. "It was in the back seat of my truck, behind the seat. I had money in there they stole, and somebody might have pissed me off at work that day. I screwed up." He also told Prothero that R. J. had helped with the death of Coffield. R. J. even stood near and snapped pictures of Gary having sex with Coffield before her murder. And as Gary strangled the sixteen-year-old, he flew into such a fit of rage and aggression, he broke Coffield's arm and strangled her.

And when he brought her to the Green River to dump her body, some part of him hoped she'd be found, and he'd be caught. Tears ran down his face in a wash of emotion. He set her into the cold watery current. "After I killed her. I was kneeling on the riverbank . . . holding her across my lap . . . I was crying, mad, upset."

In the blue-collar area of Kent County, Wendy Coffield's murder was written off as a singular horrible tragedy. A moment in the news. Her life of running away and prostitution were the causes, and her death was a tragic singular event. The locals believed they were safe as long as they didn't practice such reckless behavior, so they continued without concern. In their minds, bad things happened to people who chose dangerous activities. It wasn't long until the fisherman returned to the river, and kids continued to bike down the trails.

Of course, Wendy Coffield was only the start.

In the second week of July, Gary picked up Gisele Lovvorn. It was a Saturday evening when Lovvorn left her apartment, mentioning she planned to go out to look for about three or four tricks. She was seventeen with long thick blonde hair and a light dusting of freckles. Standing at barely five feet five inches, she weighed less than one hundred and twenty pounds. She had recently moved to the Seattle area from California after her boyfriend, James Tindal, encouraged her to move. While she came from a middle-class family, she had a bit of a rebellious streak, dropped out of school, and ran away.

She was supposed to meet her boyfriend that evening at his airport cab stand. But to Tindal's horror, he found out she'd vanished and taken nothing except for her small clutch, which she kept a knife and condoms in for work.

The night of July 17th, she had walked along the highway. The headlights of a pick-up truck lit up behind her as it pulled over. The kind face of Gary Ridgway met hers. She climbed into the truck after the initial offer was made and it was established he wasn't a cop. There was no reason to be scared. Gary was approachable and nonthreatening, and on top of it all, in the back seat was Gary Ridgway's unassuming seven-year-old son, Matthew. They drove to an isolated area off the highway between an old cemetery and the rundown Tyee Golf Course. Lovvorn provided Gary with the instructions for the location. The truck stopped. Gary turned in the front seat and looked back at Matthew.

He told his son to wait in the truck while he and Lovvorn went for a bit of a walk.

Gisele Lovvorn and Gary got out of the truck and walked a bit into the dark, quiet woods. She began to perform oral on him, and then he turned her around to have sex with her from behind. Gary climaxed with her on her hands and knees and then asked, "Is that my son coming?"

Lovvorn lifted her head to look up and back. With her neck extended, Gary hooked his right arm around her throat and began choking her. After she passed out, he pulled his black dress socks off and tied them around her throat, tightening more and more. His teeth gritted together as he pulled. He had to ensure she was dead. He tried to untie the dress socks, worried about losing them since they were a quality pair of socks, but the knot was too tight. Finished, he left her body and returned to the truck with Matthew waiting patiently. He told his son the woman had decided to walk home.

As James Tindal waited, he became increasingly worried. He phoned the police and hospitals. None had seen or heard about Gisele Lovvorn, and none seemed to care. He called her parents, who were pleased to learn that she was no longer with Tindal. Lovvorn was a stubborn and independent woman. Still, the following day, Tindal attempted to file a missing persons report with the police, but they didn't believe her disappearance was cause for concern. No report was filed. He returned, and this time created such a scene, they finally filed one.

But they told him she'd eventually turn up. They figured she'd gotten in a fight and ran off.

With no help, Tindal drove for the next several weeks. Her photo clutched in his hand, hoping for some answer or clue on where she was. He began to think some pimps kidnapped her, but the trails grew cold, and the police were little help.

Tindal reached out to a psychic he knew from Idaho. He gave her one of Lovvorn's vests. It was his last hope. The psychic clasped the vest for a moment then set it aside. "Well, she's dead. She's lying face down without any clothes on, in mud. There's a big tangle of bushes next to her. I think they're like briar bushes. Something's around her throat. And she is not in water," she told Tindal.

"Can you give me a better location?" he asked.

"She's not far from home."

A tangle of bushes near the Strip could be anywhere, Tindal learned. And his hope of finding Lovvorn was lost.

He stopped his search for his girlfriend, and the missing person report remained untouched by the police.

But by August 1982, all their attention was focused on the cold, cool water of the Green River.

Signs of a Pattern

August 12, 1982, a light drizzle fell over the Green River and its surrounding forest. Frank Linard worked at PD&J Meat Company slaughterhouse. His job was to clean up the animal remains, and he'd gone out behind the slaughterhouse to do just that. He climbed atop the work truck, loading up the septic tank remains to be cleared, and while he waited, he looked out over the river. He pulled out a cigar, lit it, and relaxed. It would be a few minutes. That summer morning, the current moved slower, bending its path along the factory lot. Linard noticed a strange rise in the water where sticks poked out and white foam gathered upon a sandbar. And as he stared, he realized the foam was not normal. Far too much of it stuck to the logs than the actual speed of the current. He narrowed his eyes, studying. He assumed it was nothing more than a large animal carcass. Still, it was uncommon for one to end up in the water and be caught on a log or rock.

He jumped down from the truck. The tank was still filling up, and he had time to investigate the foam. Linard walked through the trail downtrodden by fishermen's constant use, passed the blackberry bushes, and approached the foam. Through the moving water washing over, he had a horrible realization. The strange white mass was not a dead animal but a naked woman.

Her skin was almost pure white due to being submerged in the water for an extended period. Other parts were scorched by laying under the summer sun for hours. Egg-laying insects had deposited their larvae and flitted around the body. Her hair twisted around with the current as her body swayed stuck on a raised log, and the pupils of her eyes were white.

He rushed back to the slaughterhouse, grabbed the phone, and called the police. It wasn't long until the word traveled among the workers, and they emptied the building to come and see the dead woman floating in Green River.

Detective David Reichert arrived after an hour of the discovery. The parking lot was full of police cars and reporters. Reichert was a younger detective, only in his early thirties with shining blue eyes and wavy dark hair. He'd grown up in this area, and like Gary, had explored the woods as a kid. He looked over the body and spoke with the police on the scene. No blood was visible nor an apparent wound. But the woman had many tattoos. To the pathologist, it was evident several weeks had passed since her death. Gaining any fingerprint would prove almost impossible. The insects had caused damage, and the skin on her hands was beginning to melt away. Her body was placed into a blue plastic bag as television crews gathered at the crime scene. The cameras were pulled out as the whirl of a helicopter overhead hummed.

The second body had been found in the river.

The police scanned the area looking for some clue of who this woman was or how she ended up in the river. But there was nothing.

Back at the station, Detective Reichert sat at his desk. He knew that if this woman had been killed, it would be the second murder found in the Green River in less than a month. But there was no clear connection between this woman and the death of Wendy Coffield. Six months prior, he had investigated the death of Leann Wilcox, though she wasn't found in the river like the other two. Wilcox had been a friend of Coffield's as well as a prostitute. She'd been strangled too.

The identity of this third woman needed to be answered.

The following day the autopsy began. The tattoo of a heart, though now distorted, could still be made out. It read Duby—a nickname. Her lungs were clear of water, which meant she had not drowned. But she had suffocated, at least been strangled. Prints and photos were taken and brought to the department's criminal identification section, and within hours, they matched Deborah Lynn Bonner. She was a twenty-two-year-old prostitute with a record and, at times, went by Pam Peek. In the last month, she'd had several arrests under other names—all for prostitution.

Three weeks ago, Deborah had gone missing. She'd always had a wild side her whole life, but her relationship with Carl Martin had begun a series of problems. Her parents bailed her and Martin out of the Tacoma jail, and then she disappeared. Carl Martin called her parents, wondering if they had seen her. When Deborah's mom went to make a missing persons report, the police wouldn't take it. Concern filled Ms. Bonner; she believed her daughter and Martin owed a dangerous man several thousand dollars for drugs. Before her disappearance, Deborah confided in a bartender her situation. "She was crying and upset," the bartender recalled. "She didn't know how she was going to pay him." This man had threatened to kill Deborah if Martin couldn't pay his debt.

It would send the police after two solid leads and also in the wrong direction.

The last time Deborah was seen was July 25, precisely eighteen days before she was found face down in the water. She was with some friends and told them that she "planned to catch some dates." She walked out of the Three Bears Motel on the Pacific Highway South in King County, never to be seen again.

While out, she was picked up by Gary Ridgway and taken away. He would later tell his defense attorney that R. J. was a part of her death. The day after finding her, Detective Reichert arrived at the doorstep of Deborah Bonner's mother. He stepped into the rundown home. It was clear to him that these were people who had unfairly struggled through life. He brought the news of Bonner's death, and her mother grieved, broken by the horrible news. "I will not give up," Reichert told her. "I promise you, I will not give up."

It was a promise he would carry through—a promise that would take twenty years. For Reichert, it was the start of an arduous and intense investigation.

The police spoke to two hundred people, stopping bartenders, taxi drivers, family, and friends. But there were no answers.

All the while, Gary continued seemingly innocent. He spent what time he could with his son. Matthew rode in the child seat of a bike as they peddled along the Green River, stopping to share snacks and sit on the steep hills. Some of Matthew's earliest memories were with his father. After Gary's graveyard shift ended, he'd pick his son up from his grandmother's, and they'd grab fresh sprinkled donuts, driving to the airport together to look at the lights. "Even when I was in fourth grade when I was with soccer, he'd always, you know, be there for me," Matthew later told investigators. He never once believed his father was capable of murder. To him, Gary would "try to be a father like you see in the TV shows."

When later asked about having Matthew sitting there in the truck during one of their late-night drives while Gary killed, Gary admitted it was wrong. But then investigators asked whether he'd have killed Matthew if his son witnessed the murder.

"No, probably not," he first said. Then, "I don't know."

Bodies Submerged

Near the airport, the Strip was a hotspot for sex workers. They arrived to turn tricks, stake out areas, and waved down drivers who passed by. When a driver's attention was caught and they stopped, the woman would lean in through the window, working out a deal. Usually through a code, the customer asked if the women were dating. Once an agreed price was met, the sex worker got in the car, and they'd head to a private area, either a hotel room or a secluded spot off the highway. Payment was given, usually an average of $30 for oral sex, and a sexual service provided. The customer returned the sex worker, dropping them back off on the highway so she could continue hunting for customers. The peak business hours were between 3 p.m. and 9 p.m., when highway traffic was busiest.

Pimps, whom most of the girls referred to as their boyfriends, pumped the women full of cocaine, amphetamines, or heroin. It kept them working long hours, clouding their minds of logic or hesitation. In exchange, they were offered a loose promise of protection from "johns." Of course, there was little they could do when the women drove away.

Detective David Reichert knew that hundreds of women were working the Strip by 1982, a distance that ran about ten miles. Hundreds of new victims for this killer to pick up.

And on August 15th, the nightmare continued.

Robert Ainsworth unloaded the rubber raft from the bed of his truck. It was a warm summer afternoon, and he planned to float down the Green River to relax. He plopped into his raft by a bridge near West Valley Highway and began lazily drifting down the calm river. The water level was low that day, and Ainsworth could easily see the riverbed beneath him. He'd peer down into the river in search of anything interesting like antique bottles. He'd stop his raft and scoop it up from the river floor, toss it in his raft and continue on with a homemade hook. It was a little past noon when he drifted by the PD&J Meat Company slaughterhouse.

Floating was a calming pastime for Ainsworth, letting the current take him wherever.

But today would prove different.

Around the river's turn, Ainsworth saw a man standing near the river's edge. He was tall and well built, balding, and well into his forties. A trail ran down the grassy hill, leading up to another man sitting behind the driver's seat of a pickup truck. He appeared younger. Ainsworth hopped out of his raft and waded over.

"Catch anything?" Ainsworth asked, initiating friendly conversation. The man shook his head no.

"Found anything?" the man asked.

"Just this old singletree." Ainsworth pointed to the wood in his raft he'd scooped up earlier. The singletree was used for pioneer horse wagons.

"You know, there's an old motor right down there, a car motor, in the river under the water." Ainsworth could clearly see the hunk of metal beneath the surface; it was a submerged outboard motor.

"Yeah. I can see it right now."

The pickup truck driver shouted something out the window, and the older man headed off into the truck. They drove away, and Ainsworth returned to his raft.

Gary Ridgway sat in the old truck as they sped down the road. Adrenaline pumped through him. He'd been seen. Seen by a man floating down the river in a rubber raft. He'd returned with R. J. to the riverbank to have sex with the corpse of one of his victims. "One thing for sure, I . . . I got stopped there at the end, when the guy comin' down the river saw me and I said uh, 'Have you seen anything yet?' And that meant . . . point on I stopped killing anymore. He saw me."

Gary was done leaving bodies in the Green River.

But to Ainsworth, there was no cause for alarm. Nothing was unusual about spotting two men at the riverbank until he continued for about one minute down the river and looked over the raft's edge.

Dark hair caught his attention. Stone cold eyes stared back at him as the body bobbed with the low waves, submerged. She was small, child-like. The sight of it all was a shock, and immediately, Ainsworth reasoned it was a mannequin.

He tried to hook onto what he thought was a doll with his bottle pole, used for collecting antique bottles in the river, and as he reached out, his raft turned. It bumped something. He turned to find in horror another body. These were not mannequins; these were dead women. The realization shook him. He was approximately six hundred yards from where Deborah Bonner's body had been found.

With adrenaline shooting through his system, he reached the riverbank and headed back to where the fishermen in the truck were. But they were long gone, and Ainsworth was at a loss of what to do next.

For the next hour and a half, he waited by the roadside. Finally, a man with two children stopped. He told them about the horror that lurked in the river, and the man drove off to call the police. Ainsworth had no choice but to sit and wait.

Detective Dave Reichert had attended Sunday service that morning with his wife and children when he got the call.

"Some guy out there says he found some bodies." It had to be a bad joke, he thought. It'd only been three days since the last discovery at the slaughterhouse.

When he arrived at the scene, the yellow crime scene tape was strung across trees. The parking lot of the slaughterhouse was now filled with police vehicles. Down the steep grassy hill following the fresh trail made by the police. The tall grass enveloped him entirely as he reached the river's edge. He walked to where several other officers were gathered, looking out into the river.

The first body laid over the river floor face down, naked. Heavy rocks were placed on her foot, knee, buttocks, and shoulder. The silt carried by the river had deposited over her skin, making her race challenging to determine. Ten feet upstream, Reichert found the second body. She laid face up in the water with nothing except for a front clasping bra that was opened. Heavy rocks had been set upon her body as well, except her right hand lifted over the water as the waves bounced it back and forth. Her eyes and mouth were open as if she were reaching out, waiting to be found. They were meant to remain submerged, but as gas filled the corpses, they could no longer be ignored. As Reichert inspected the scene, his complete focus went into studying. He wondered how the killer brought two bodies down the hill. It was rather steep, and the grass was slippery terrain. Whoever their killer was, it was clear he was strong.

This was a hot spot for anglers, and cans, cigarette buds, and other garbage littered the ground. Reichert moved through the steep bank, searching for any more evidence, any hint of who this killer could be. Through the five-foot-tall underbrush, he stepped carefully, unable to see farther than a few steps ahead of himself. His focus shifted down to in front of him about halfway up the bank. Within the tall, thick grass, another female corpse laid stiff, face down and dead before him.

"I've got another one!" he shouted to the nearby police. Her legs stuck out straight, with her heels almost touching. She appeared young, in her mid-teens, and her skin was sunburned from laying outside for hours. Around her neck, a pair of blue jeans tied tightly—just like Wendy Coffield. But her body had never been touched by the river water and could only have been lying face down in the dirt for a few days. Her white bra was pulled up, exposing her breasts and a multitude of bruises covered her skin.

Reichert immediately wondered why this body had been dumped in the brush and not made it to the river with the others. The killer might have been scared off by someone approaching, leaving her here hidden in the grass.

The three women discovered that day had all died from probable asphyxiation.

The bodies were pulled from the river, bloated and disfigured. It was not an easy task as the skin simply slid off from being submerged. One body had been in the water for about a week, and the other no longer than three or four days. The third corpse found on the steep hill was still undergoing rigor mortis; that meant she'd only been dead about a day or two.

Horror shook them. It was like Ted Bundy all over again, dead women scattered through the woods. And these were hidden well, meant to be disguised. From the road, it would be near impossible to spot these women.

The following day, the headline of *Seattle Post-Intelligencer* read: 3 DEAD WOMEN FOUND IN, NEAR GREEN RIVER.

Green River
Task Force

Detective David Kraske formed the Green River Task Force on August 16th. There were twenty-five investigators from King County, the Seattle Police Department, the Tacoma Police Department, and the Kent Police Department. The largest force assembled to date. None of which were prepared for the horror that laid ahead. Five young women had been found, dead all within a month's time. There was another lethal killer on the loose, one that the police were clueless on where to begin.

They had no witnesses, aside from Ainsworth, who only had a vague description of the two men near the riverbank. The victims hadn't been identified, and no evidence was found on the river.

The same day the task force was assembled, the medical examiner got the details on the three bodies. It was concluded all three had been asphyxiated. Semen was discovered in two of the bodies, and the rocks that pinned them down were from the land. But more telling of the crimes' nature was the discovery of fist-sized stones shoved inside the vaginas of the two in the river.

When later asked by Detective Jensen why Gary inserted rocks into the two women, he struggled to explain or provide a clear answer. First, he told them it had been R. J.'s idea. Then later, when asked a second time, he said, "Uh . . . um . . . might be symbolic. The woman would not have sex with anybody else. But I don't know. Keep anybody else from having sex. And you know not . . . not that they would because her . . . she's dead. But just to . . . just to . . . somethin' that I wanted to do. So I started on her. I was gonna do it."

"Was it something that you'd thought of before, or . . . ?" Detective Tom Jensen asked.

"Yeah, I thought of it just when I got there. Had sex. There's a . . . there's a rock. I'll put it in her vagina."

And while Gary would never reveal or understand his own motives behind the strange action, detectives knew that these murders had a twisted sexual nature. Their killer was making a statement about prostitutes and himself.

It was also clear their killer planned. The first two women had been placed in the river and floated away, but he began weighing them down after the initial discovery. They knew then he was watching the news, reading the newspaper, and paying attention. And Gary was. He became obsessive over not being caught and hiding his evidence. When he picked up his future dates, he was sure to wear gloves and knew to move around the area, finding new dumpsites.

Still, the police put the river under strict surveillance.

While the news and stories spread, there was little fear among the Kent County community. These murders were happening to prostitutes and runaways, which society viewed as the untouchables. It had little effect on them.

Some of the women who continued working as prostitutes moved to Portland, California, and Las Vegas. Others, who stayed in Seattle, started working downtown since the Strip was the targeted area. But many of them continued walking around the airport area, waiting for businessmen who came in for the weekend and locals.

When they were instructed to stay off the streets, the warning was treated as nothing more than a joke. The need for food, shelter, and drug money outweighed the haunting fear of murder. Every time they climbed into the car of a stranger, they knew they were risking their safety. But what choice did they have? Most assumed they'd had enough experience to sniff out the killer. A false security of their "street sense" would be enough to protect them. And if they did manage to slip into the mad man's hands, they were prepared. The women revealed the knives, mace, guns, and other weapons they were ready to use if it came to life and death to the reporters who swarmed the streets for answers.

They answered the police's questions, who were working to identify the three women found on August 15th. But the pimps and sex workers were hesitant to trust the police. Rarely the whole truth was told. They moved along the Strip, showing photos, hoping someone might recognize a face. They compiled what little forensic evidence they could. The river had destroyed much of it. And with each day that passed, the trail of the killer grew colder.

The media frenzy created confusion as news reporters outnumbered the police on the Strip. As the police conducted interviews, they were unsure whether the stories were coming from the television or personal experience. "It's been the sheer number of reporters on every scene in connection with this story that has us overwhelmed," the police press spokesman, Pat Ferguson, said. "They have been reaching witnesses and acquaintances of witnesses and the victims before we had a chance to get to them." The media withdrew their teams shortly after Ferguson's statement, but the damage had been done.

The first woman pulled from the river on August 15th to be identified was Marcia Chapman, known as Tiny by her friends for being petite and having a lovely, youthful face. The thirty-one-year-old was the mother to three young children whom she loved and supported by sex work. She worked in the area near the Seattle-Tacoma International Airport and lived in a close apartment with her kids.

Unlike many of the other prostitutes, Chapman was independent and didn't work for a pimp. She once told a neighbor, "Why should I give the money to a man? I need it for my kids, not for some man."

So, on August 1, 1982, around 8:30 p.m., when Marcia stepped out of her front door, she told her children she was running to the store. The store wasn't on the agenda. Instead, she was picked up by Gary Ridgway, never to be seen again.

Marcia Chapman, Deborah Bonner, and Wendy Coffield may have known one another, and all of the first five victims discovered were known to work in the same area.

Unlike Chapman, the second woman identified, Cynthia Hinds, known as "Cookie," had a pimp to protect her. He watched her climb into a black jeep with a man on August 11th. She had been waiting outside the convenience store. And when she was out of her pimp's sight, there was nothing he could do to save her. She had been picked up only twelve blocks from where Chapman had vanished.

Hinds had a run-in with Gary.

Opal Charmaine Mills was the third woman to be identified. The girl was barely sixteen years old when she was left hidden among the tall reeds. Barely over five feet tall, she had a bright smile and parents who loved her. "I've read the things in the newspaper," said Robert Mills, Opal's father, "and she just didn't fit in. My little kids have had everything." He was sure his daughter had never gotten involved with prostitution, but her friends said otherwise.

According to the Mills, their daughter was close friends with a woman known as "Cookie." They had left together on August 11th, the day Deborah's body was discovered, to paint apartments. Opal told her family she'd inquire about getting her brother a job painting as well. On August 12th, at 12:55 p.m., Opal Mills picked up the telephone in a phone booth to call her parents from Angle Lake State Park, near the Strip. She let them know there were no other job opportunities and was never heard from again. Three days later, Detective Reichert would stumble over her body near the blackberry bushes.

The Thursday after she'd made the call, she was picked up by Ridgway and her body dumped in the grassland.

With all the bodies identified, police noticed that three of the first five were high school age, and the other two were physically small. The killer was picking up women who were weak and vulnerable.

Gary may have taken Hinds and Mills to the old, abandoned barn and gotten drunk. There he and R. J. raped and strangled them. "When I woke up, R. J. was the only one there. R. J. showed me pictures they had taken of me having sex with the black prostitute. They had taken pictures of me with my hands around her neck. She was naked, and her eyes were closed. She looked dead. R. J. told me she was dead." When he came to and sobered up, R. J. recounted Gary's activities. "R. J. told me they had pictures of me with two dead prostitutes. They were both black ladies. One had pants around their neck, and one didn't."

Around midnight, they took the bodies to the Green River and set them in.

An accomplice working with Gary made sense. Opal Mills was found with two loads of DNA inside of her. Carrying the bodies down the steep hill into the river would have required immense strength as well as the massive heavy rocks that pressed their bodies beneath the water. "I took pictures of Hinds and Chapman. I went back with a Polaroid and took pictures." He later said these pictures were thrown in the river.

And when Ainsworth floated down that river that day to find the bodies of Hinds and Chapman, he saw Gary Ridgway standing at the riverbank with another man waiting in a car.

Gary Ridgway admitted to returning to the bodies before leaving them in the river. He had sex with the corpses of Hinds and Chapman, and when he was finished, he returned to place them in the river. The urges began with Coffield and worsened each time. He'd returned for Opal Mills but had been scared off by Ainsworth.

Trail Gone Cold

To the investigators, the rest of August was moving on without any new incident or discovery. They began to build connections between the five river victims. Coffield and Mills attended the same junior high school. Chapman and Hinds worked in the same area and were known to sit at the bar together. Coffield, Bonner, and Chapman were addicted to cocaine and heroin. The connections were too similar to be ignored. Whoever this killer was, they clearly frequented the same spot, and perhaps if the police spoke with the other prostitutes, they could uncover information about these five women's clients.

Undercover cops were sent out to bars in the surrounding area, but there was no information leading them to the killer. They asked if anyone had experienced weird kinky demands or received any strange threats, but no one had answers. No connections to missing sex workers could be made. Like Lovvorn, whose body waited on the cold ground to be discovered, too many of the women went missing for it to stand out.

But the Green River Task Force knew their killer would strike again.

One woman told the police she'd had a strange encounter with a client. Picked up in Seattle's central region, the driver took her toward the river. He told her that if she didn't listen, then she'd end up like "those other bitches they found." But the man's car broke down at a traffic light, and she was able to open the door and escape. And when asked who this man was, she replied she didn't know. He was average-looking.

They knew the potential victims would be their best witnesses, but the sex workers had little trust in the police. Many had been arrested during undercover operations. They were unreliable, and not all came forward. Not until much later.

August 22, 1982. It was late in the summer night. Twenty-one-year-old Susan Widmark was picked up by a man driving a blue and white pickup truck in the central area of Seattle. They spoke briefly, and the man agreed to pay for oral sex. Widmark got into the truck and started to provide directions to a nearby house.

But the man did not listen. Instead, his foot stomped hard on the gas pedal. The outside world passed at high speed as they raced down the Pacific Highway South.

"If you don't want to get hurt, you'll do what I tell you." He pointed a pistol at her head, and the truck veered off onto a dirt road. In a dark, isolated area, the man parked the vehicle. While keeping the pistol pointed at her head, he ordered her to strip down and then he raped her.

Fear built inside of Widmark. With the act finished, she began to dress, but the man stopped her.

"You don't have to bother with that. You won't be working anymore tonight, anyway," he said. "Haven't you heard about all those hookers they found in the river?"

She told him that she didn't understand. He laughed and turned the ignition. They were headed straight to the riverbank. The cold metal pistol remained pointed directly at her.

It was a stoplight when the man's hand wavered slightly. Widmark took the opportunity to leap from the car half-naked into the dark summer night. The truck sped off, but not before she turned and memorized part of the license plate and vehicle's make.

Adrenaline pumped through her system. Upset and scared, she managed to hitchhike her way back to the Pacific Highway South and her pimp. She told him the story, but he did not want to tell the police about her brief dance with death.

A month later, the police would interview Widmark, only to be led to a man named Charles Clinton Clark. After speaking with Clark, they realized this was indeed not their killer.

Unknowingly, Gary's dark acts of murder and rape had only begun to inspire others to act out on their violent urges. The police were not one step closer to finding the average forty-year-old who moved in the world invisible to the police.

On August 29, 1982, Gary was out by his pickup truck on South 192nd Street. Four bodies would be discovered in this area a year later. It was around 1 a.m. when the Port of Seattle Police spotted him. He told the officers he had pulled over to urinate, and they let him go without any other questions. They had no idea they'd let the Green River Killer walk away.

The End of Summer.
The Start of the Silent Killer

August 29, 1982. It was Sunday, and Gary had the day off. He cruised along the Strip.

Sixteen-year-old Terry Renee Milligan decided to take a break from the streets and headed back to the motel she currently lived in with her boyfriend. It was located on South 144th Street and Pacific Highway South. At 6 p.m., she left for the local Wendy's to grab some dinner about five blocks away. She said goodbye to her boyfriend and walked out into the late summer evening.

That was the last time she was seen alive.

Gary pulled up beside the teenager, and the terms of a "date" were struck. She opened the car door, convinced there was nothing to fear about Gary. He stepped on the gas pedal, heading to the exact same place he brought Lovvorn. In the desolate, empty area, they had intercourse, and Gary strangled her. Initially, he planned to leave her body, but that wouldn't work. Two boys in the forest witnessed Gary and Milligan together. It was too much of a risk.

He loaded her body back into the truck and drove to Star Lake, laying her body in the dirt and grass at the base of a hill. His hands scrambled as he panicked. The witnesses had him worried. Milligan's blue blouse was left with her body as Gary drove home. The need for sex, for ownership of his victims, pushed him to return the following day. He had sex with her corpse, but because rigor mortis had begun, he had to pry her legs apart, leaving them at a ninety-degree angle.

September 15, 1982. Two weeks after Milligan disappeared from the streets, Mary Meehan stepped out onto Pacific Highway South. Bright headlights passed by as potential customers scoped her out. She was seven months pregnant but carried it in such a way it didn't discourage any clients. Around 9 p.m., a pickup truck slowed down, and Meehan agreed to go on a date with Gary Ridgway. They arrived at the Sandstone Motel. But instead of enjoying the privacy of the motel, Gary suggested they walk a few blocks to have sex outdoors.

They walked together to a secluded forest area, where tall trees cast dark shadows around them. There Meehan began to perform oral, but Gary became enraged when she refused to have vaginal sex. He later told investigators that he was "paying for the vagina." Angry, resentment began to build, and Gary couldn't get an erection. In a fit of rage, he jumped behind Meehan, wrapping his arm around her throat, and killed her. The silence of the woods fell around him.

The initial swell of rage subsided as he realized he'd killed her far too close to the road. Someone driving by might see her body.

Gary returned to his truck and pulled out a shovel. He decided to dig a shallow grave and bury her there. He removed her clothing and jewelry then shoveled dirt back over her still-warm body. He confessed to investigators that he was unaware of her pregnancy, but it would have changed nothing if he had known. He still would have killed her. She was eighteen at the time of her death.

When the news of the Green River murders made its way to the Estes's home, Tom and Carol Estes became worried sick because their daughter Debbie was a runaway, and they knew she was working the streets. For the past several months, Debbie's parents reported their daughter missing, but they were told the police could do little. They didn't know that their daughter was working under the name "Betty Lorraine Jones" and had been arrested four times for prostitution. And while Tom and Carol persisted in asking the police about their daughter, the officers had no way nor cared to link Betty Jones to Debbie. They were clueless their daughter was turning tricks right across from their office.

She'd had her fair share of troubled run-ins with dangerous men, so she was prepared for the worst.

On August 30th, under the persona of Betty Jones, Debbie Estes had seventy-five dollars on her and had no intention of working that day. She wanted to go shopping at the mall. Around 4 p.m., a man in a blue and white pickup truck pulled up to Estes and offered her a ride. She agreed. But after several minutes, the ride to the mall became dangerous. The man pulled out a pistol. A frightened Estes stared down the metal barrel of the gun aimed directly at her.

"I won't use this," he said, "if you do what I say. Take off your blouse." She refused, and he pulled back the hammer of the pistol. Debbie removed her blouse as the fear mounted. The truck came to a stop after the driver veered off onto an empty dirt road. He next instructed her to take off her blue jeans. "Give me a blow job," he demanded.

Debbie refused again and was immediately struck with the pistol. Petrified and scared for her life, she performed oral. And when it was over, the man bound her hands behind her back and stole her money. With the gun pointed at her back, he led her deeper into the woods, untying her hands. He told her to wait a while as he walked away. Alone, Debbie stood in the forest until she heard the truck's engine drive down the road. She sprinted to a nearby home, asking for help, and called the police.

Now, they had a lead. And after Susan Widmark's similar encounter, they were able to narrow it down to Charles Clinton Clark. Debbie Estes worked with the police, showing them where Clark drove and raped her in the woods. She was willing to testify in court against him. But like so many others, Clark would prove to be a fruitless lead. After showing the police where she was raped, a detective dropped her off at the Stevenson Motel around 3 p.m. on September 20th.

It was the last time she'd ever be seen alive.

After helping investigators hunt down Clark, Debbie Estes was picked up by Gary Ridgway and strangled to death that night. He tied her clothing around her neck, ensuring she was dead, then buried her body in a construction site in Federal Way. Later Gary would make a strange comment to his coworker Gary Yager about how a construction site would make a good place to dump a body. Debbie Estes, known as "muffin" by her parents, was only fifteen years old when she was killed.

Six days later, it was a Saturday evening when a man arrived south of the airport to ride around on his dirt bike. He had the day off, and the sandy abandoned lots were perfect for riding around on. As he drove around the base of a hillock, a horrible rotting scent filled his nose. He stopped, inhaling. The smell did not dissipate. In fact, it grew more pungent.

He cut the engine of the dirt bike and followed the intense smell to some blackberry bushes. He pushed back the foliage to discover a young woman's dead body half-hidden in the abandoned yard and well into decomposing. Sick to his stomach and horrified, the biker stepped back. No one would have found the body, blocked from traffic surrounded by overgrown lots, cement, and vacant homes.

The police arrived to find the body naked, face-up, legs spread apart, and a pair of men's black socks knotted tightly around her neck.

The following morning, detectives met with a medical examiner.

A light rain drizzled in the early fall morning. The brush had been cleared away, and investigators gathered what they could of the mostly decomposed remains, placing them in a blue body bag. But no other trace evidence or personal belongings was found.

Search dogs scoured the lots looking for any more bodies or evidence, but still, the search came up empty-handed.

Detectives were reasonably confident they knew who the dead woman was. They remembered a cab driver, worried about his girlfriend. He described a bird tattoo on her breast, just like the one this dead woman had. Dental records confirmed the theory, but it was Tindal's psychic who had been right. Gisele Lovvorn was not in the water, but only a few miles from home, laying among the bushes. The circumstances of her death, her age, and the time she was killed meant that the Green River Killer had ended six lives.

As investigators pulled Lovvorn from the bushes, Gary drove, searching for his next victim.

Linda Rule was sixteen years old on September 26th. She was headed down to the K-Mart on Aurora and 130th Street in North Seattle. Gary had been in the county and stopped at an ATM. He withdrew $50, and

at some point, that day, picked Linda Rule up. "We were just drivin'
around," he later told investigators during an interview, "and found a
vacant lot in front of the hospital and had a date, and I killed her there,
outside the … truck." From behind, he wrapped his hands around her
throat, and when she was dead, he went through her pockets, taking what
he could. He found matches and lit her hair on fire twice but worried
someone might see the smoke. When asked why he lit her hair on fire,
he later said, "That would excite me to see her … um … she had beautiful
hair and to hurt her more."

Taking away what these women valued gave Gary great pleasure. He
stole from them once he took their lives. He believed they were unworthy
of jewelry, money, or beauty. Their clothing he'd toss out the window
after he left their bodies.

As September pushed into October, the number of sex workers on
the Strip started to decline, and the police had found no new bodies. The
police pursued a man named Melvyn Foster, whom Detective Reichert
firmly believed was their prime suspect. He was nothing more than a car
thief who enjoyed paying teenage girls for sex, and in the spring of 1982,
Foster had encountered Marcia Chapman, Wendy Coffield, Cynthia
Hinds, Debbie Bonner, and Opal Mills.

While the police watched Foster's every move, the bodies stopped
coming in. That meant they'd either found their killer, or he had gone
into hiding. But there was another fear. The Green River Killer hadn't
stopped. He'd only learned to evade them.

Rose Hahn and her husband began moving out of Ridgway's home
in the fall of 1982, where they had been living since April. He spent the
summer and early fall away most evenings, only to pop in once in a while
to use the kitchen or bathroom. Oftentimes, he was out washing his
maroon truck with a white canopy top. He loved to keep his truck

looking nice, constantly cleaning and washing it. The Hahns moved out on October 2, 1982.

There was no one around to pry or overhear. Gary was free to bring whomever through the front door.

On October 8, 1982, Denise Bush stayed at the Moonrise Motel with a friend near 144th Street. She and her pimp sat in the room, flipping a coin to see who would go out and get the next pack of cigarettes. She lost. Defeated, she tossed on a hoodie and a pair of jeans and left.

Gary had been off work that day for an eye ailment. He spent $26 on gas at a gas station near the Moonrise Motel.

Denise Bush's friend saw her and a strange man speaking at the 7-Eleven across from the motel the night before. She described the man as five foot ten and in his early thirties. He wore a blue plaid shirt with jeans and drove a dull green GMC pickup truck. The truck's hood was up, and the man stood beside it, but something about his behavior tipped the friend off. Immediately, she became weary of the stranger talking to Bush. His eyes flickered up. When he saw her watching, he ducked his head behind the hood.

Later, Denise's friend asked who that man was. She danced around the question, only mentioning they would be meeting later.

The green truck didn't match Gary's at the time, but it was similar to his brother's. Bush's friend would later select Gary's picture as the strange man she saw that evening.

Gary often parked at that 7-Eleven, flipping the hood of his truck up. He'd check the oil and look for prostitutes there. Sometimes, the woman would get into his car right there. Other times a new meeting place would be set for later. And though Ridgway assumed the 7-Eleven workers knew he was there to pick up prostitutes, he continued to use the location to scout out his next victims. Denise had been one of them.

On October 8th, Gary picked up Bush and took her to Tukwila. While having sex with her, he strangled her with his arm. She screamed, trying to fight back. With twisted delight, Gary promised he'd let her go if she stopped screaming. It was a promise he never intended to keep. He left her body where he killed her, covering it with plastic.

The day after Denise vanished, seventeen-year-old Shawnda Summers was picked up by Gary. There were no witnesses to her disappearance, and it took several weeks before her father filed a missing person report and her mother arrived from California to hopefully find her. Still, there was no hope in their search. Gary had picked the teenage girl up and strangled her to death. His legs wrapped tightly around her body to keep her still as he choked the life out of her.

Shirley Sherrill started sex work in the summer of 1982 as Gary began his killing career. She was eighteen years old when she disappeared from the streets. Her pimp couldn't quite recall the exact date he last saw her. Between October 20th to the 22nd, he dropped Sherrill off at Seattle's International District in the morning. It was another prostitute who watched Sherrill at four in the afternoon speaking with two white men in a black pickup truck.

It would be a year before her mother called to report her daughter missing.

The Only
One to Escape

Gary had fallen into an addiction to murder. During an interview, he'd later confess that his problem with prostitutes had a similar effect on him as "the way alcohol does an alcoholic." His anger was uncontrollable, and in his mind, he was doing the area a service by ridding the world of prostitutes.

November 9, 1982, Gary's maroon-colored pickup truck pulled up beside Rebecca Garde. She had been hitchhiking and now waited at a bus stop along the Pacific Highway South. They began to chat, and Gary told Garde that he'd been arrested that day in a vice operation, and his son was being taken from him. He played the empathy card, and discussing his son made him relatable. Wearing shorts, high knee socks, and tennis shoes, nothing was threatening about him.

They set the price of a car date at $20, and Garde hopped in. It was a quick way to catch a ride out of Seattle's rain and pay for some marijuana. To her, Gary appeared to be nothing more than "boring" and "dull." Though, she noticed his hands were large and his eyes beady. That was what she remembered the most. "I remember the look in his eyes," she later recalled. She asked him if he was the Green River Killer, and he assured her he wasn't. "I acted in a way with the prostitutes to make them feel that more comfortable and got in their comfort zone. Here is a guy, not muscle-bound ordinary John, and yet that was their downfall. My appearance was different from what I really was." Her fear eased when he revealed his identification for the Kenworth Trucking Co.

Garde was unaware that the man she directed away from the highway was eagerly waiting to attack her. Beneath the exterior of a harmless father, Gary stopped the car and got out, asking if they could head to the woods for a bit. Garde agreed and she followed him into the forest, where the dense trees and thick foliage kept the light out.

Gary stopped walking when he climbed up a sharp incline and removed his shorts, dropping them to his ankles. Garde kept her clothes on as she bent down on her knees and performed oral sex. The whole time she noticed, Ridgway failed to have an erection.

"You bitch, you bit my cock!" He suddenly began screaming. She later told the police this was not true. Gary pushed hard, whipped Garde around, and placed his arms in a tight chokehold around her neck, squeezing. He used his weight to force her to the ground, and when she was helpless, he wrapped his hands around her neck and began suffocating her.

Panic and adrenaline surged through Garde. She twisted beneath Ridgway and rolled to face him, now his hands tightened around the front of her neck, crushing her throat. There was no doubt in her mind that this man had every intention of taking her life then and there. His grip was unbearably tight to the point Garde could not scream. "All of a sudden, he starts grabbing me, and we're rolling all over the place," she described. "He tried covering my mouth and my nose, and I just kept trying to breathe. He smothered me on the ground. ... He was sitting on top of me." And even though she could only plea for her life, she decided she would not die that night.

Through a weak voice, she told him about how she cared for her mother. It was then, Gary released his grip slightly. Perhaps the mention of her mother struck a chord of empathy within Gary because it was then Garde pushed him against a tree. It was as if he was trapped in a daze with his pants still draped at his ankles. Sprinting down the hill, Rebecca found a mobile home in the nearby trailer park.

In a frantic state, she pounded on the door over and over until it opened.

"Please help me!"

The trailer owner saw her torn blouse and the skin around her neck, bruised and red.

Gary put his clothes back on after watching Garde disappear into a trailer. He walked back to his truck and drove away. She would wait two years to approach the police with her story out of fear of her previous drug use and prostitution.

By mid-November, no new bodies had been discovered and other crimes were being committed. Left at a multitude of dead ends, the Green River Task Force was reassigned to other duties. David Reichert was the only one left as a detective on the case.

Cold Winter of Death

"Well, I had so much uh, hate in my, in myself that, that I'd uh . . . 'cause I had a lot of things I didn't stand up for," Gary said. "So I . . . I dated a woman. If she would have sex—if it was a motel or whatever—if she . . . lied to me about . . . anything, or hurrying me and not enjoying the sex, um . . . a culmination of all those, or, or some of 'em, uh, during the middle. And . . . and a lot of 'em were over by the airport—the, the uh, noise set me off. I know one of 'em . . . like a truck came by and, and it set me off. And plus, the, the woman lyin' to me."

The fall turned to cold winter.

December 2, 1982, the phone rang inside Rebecca Marrero's apartment. Her family overheard parts of the conversation. The voice on the other line wanted Marrero to go somewhere, but when she refused, an argument ensued. Marrero slammed the phone down and asked her family to watch her three-year-old. She had to head out but failed to mention where. She took a bath, left her mother's, and the following day,

Marrero rented a room at the Western Six Motel. Gary killed her the night of December 3rd. Her body wouldn't be found for another twenty-eight years later in 2010.

December 24, 1982, Colleen Brockman was fifteen years old when she made plans to meet with a friend at the Greyhound Bus Station. They'd rented a room at a nearby motel earlier and planned to arrive around noon, but Brockman never returned.

While others celebrated the holidays with family, Gary drove that Christmas Eve. He stopped and picked up the young Brockman north of Chinatown. They began to have sex in the back of his truck when he strangled her. She begged to go, and Gary reassured her, "Don't fight. I'm not gonna … I'll let you go." Then he pressed his foot against her throat and ended her life. He drove to Jovita Boulevard and dragged her body twenty feet away from the road to leave her corpse. "Yeah, I picked her up in Chinatown and killed her in my truck. I think she had braces," he'd later say in an interview.

But that Christmas Eve, Gary wasn't finished with his blood lust. He picked up twenty-year-old Sandra Major. She was last seen climbing into a truck near North 90th Street and Aurora Avenue North. When he finished killing her, Gary drove near a cemetery on Mountainview Drive and left her body there on the hillside. It was a destination he'd thought about earlier. He passed by the cemetery many times on his way to work from the home he and Marcia shared. He described it as, "There's a fantastic bank and trees. Just an excellent place to dump a woman, and I can see ahead when I drop her off."

At the end of January 1983, a construction worker laid down water pipes in a shallow ditch near the Northgate Hospital. In the winter air, he began removing overgrown brush that laid in the way. He lifted the branches, horrified to discover a human skeleton staring back at him in the cold earth. Linda Rule's body had been found.

The winter months continued, and the detectives were left in silence.

It is unknown if Gary killed during this time, but Matthew fondly remembered his father pulling over one day while out on a drive when he was seven or eight years old. Gary jumped out of the car to help at the scene of an accident. Matthew watched as his good Samaritan father pulled out an army surplus blanket from the trunk to drape over the accident victims. It came from the trunk that had hauled so many victims.

But these acts of kindness did nothing to rectify Gary's true nature.

March 3rd, Alma Smith's friend, Cynthia Basset-Ornelas, returned from picking up johns. The best friends vowed to watch out for each other as they worked the streets. Alma had been seeing Ridgway before and dated him on several occasions at his home. He often dated a woman several times. He knew it helped establish a good rapport with the girls. If they came back paid and unharmed, they'd tell their other sex workers, Ridgway was safe and could be trusted.

Ornelas had only been gone with a client for forty-five minutes. Upon returning, she assumed Smith wouldn't be gone long and was most likely with a client at the moment. On that particular night, Gary had gotten off work at 3:20 in the afternoon. He lived only three miles from where Alma was last seen. That day, he'd borrowed his brother's blue Dodge pickup truck.

While her roommate worried sick over Smith's disappearance, Gary Ridgway had taken her to his home. It only took him an hour once inside his home. In his bed, they began to have sex when he strangled her. There was no mess to clean up this time, and so he decided after dumping her body at Star Lake, he could easily pick up another victim. He returned to the Red Lion Inn parking lot.

Ornelas saw the white and blue truck and thought Smith was inside and dating the man. She walked over and peered into the car window, hoping to find her friend. All she saw was Gary Ridgway, who looked her over and then asked what she wanted.

"Not you." Ornelas turned around and walked away, worried. Ridgway got out of the car and began following Ornelas. She was struck with a bad feeling about the encounter and told him to leave her alone. He continued following her, asking about her blonde friend. She and Smith had never worked together before, which meant he'd seen them together that very night. After she held her ground and refused to speak with Gary, he left.

Time began to pass, and there was still no sign of Smith.

"Anyone know where Alma went?" Ornelas asked anxiously to a passerby outside the Red Lion Inn where they'd been waiting.

"She left with some guy in a blue pickup truck."

"White or black?"

"White—just an average-looking guy. You know…"

Alma never showed up.

But his compulsion to kill had left him with one grave mistake. He'd left a witness behind at the Red Lion Inn. One that would not forget what happened to Alma Smith or the man in the blue truck.

Seventeen-year-old Delores Williams disappeared similarly to Alma Smith sometime in early to mid-March of 1983, outside the Red Lion Inn when Gary picked her up. He left her naked body with a rock in her pelvis at the Star Lake dumpsite.

It was six in the evening on April 10th. In his free time, Gary took his brother's truck to cruise down the Strip. He picked up Gail Matthews off the Pacific Highway South and drove home. He stopped on the road at South 216th, waiting to turn left. Gail Matthews' boyfriend, Curtis Weaver, happened to pull up beside them. They'd been out together earlier that night. Weaver saw his girlfriend, sitting in the blue-green truck with a white canopy. He waved, trying to get Gail's attention, but it appeared as though she was in a trance. Her eyes remained forward, acting as if Weaver wasn't there.

Matthews' boyfriend would never lay eyes on her again, as she would end up being the next victim dumped at Star Lake.

After her death, Gary painted his brother's truck a different color.

Several days after the murder of Gail Matthews, Andrea Childers was killed by Ridgway. He would return to have sex with the corpse on multiple occasions after leaving her body at the South Airport site. He attempted to bury her body but stopped when he realized he could be seen.

April 17th, Gary waited outside Seven-Eleven beside his truck. Seventeen-year-old Sandra Gabbert handed her boyfriend and pimp the seventy dollars cash she'd made earlier that day. She planned to go out and make a bit more. The last time she was seen was at the Seven-Eleven.

At some point that day, Gabbert climbed into the pickup and drove off with Gary, who strangled her to death. With a fresh kill, Gary returned to the Star Lake site where four other bodies laid in the dirt and brush, hidden. Gary rolled her body down the hill until it hit a log, then he began gathering brush and lost sticks to lay over the top. Finished and satisfied that Gabbert was successfully hidden, Gary headed back to the truck. A jogger sprinted by. They saw one another, but Gary cared little. He'd already done away with the body. There was no reason to panic.

That same night he would kill again.

The murder of Sandra Gabbert hadn't been enough to fill Gary's lust to kill. That night, he drove searching the streets until seventeen-year-old Kimi-Kai Pitsor caught his attention. He was desperate to kill, and even though Pitsor was walking in downtown Seattle with her pimp/boyfriend, Gary didn't care. He broke his rule of never picking up a victim with a witness present. He pulled up in the light green truck with a camper on the back, and Pitsor climbed in.

She agreed to date him at his home if he'd be willing to take her back to downtown Seattle. Gary promised he would, of course, he had no intention to follow through. "There's no way I'm going to waste my time having sex with her, pay her $40, or $30 or $60 or whatever. And then drive her all the way back into Seattle. That's something I wouldn't do. I would get her there and kill her. I'm not going to waste my money driving all the way back."

After they had sex, he murdered her in his bed and disposed of the body.

Gary's rage and his desire to regain control consumed him. He'd become a master of his craft and was propelled to kill. In his mind, these women were nothing. At his home alone, ligatures of ropes, belts, and towels were used as he learned to avoid being scratched. If they did scratch him, he knew to cut their fingernails and flush them away to avoid leaving DNA behind.

Two weeks had passed since Sandra Gabbert and Kimi-Kai Pitsor were last seen. Neither one had a missing report filed yet, and Marie Malvar worked the streets with her boyfriend Bobby Woods near the

Three Bears Motel. It was ten in the evening when Gary in his green-colored truck drove up, motioning for Malvar to join him. She went willingly, but her boyfriend followed close behind. He pulled up beside the truck and saw Malvar in a heated conversation with the man.

Gary must have noticed the boyfriend because he slammed his foot on the gas. Woods stayed close behind, accelerating to keep up with Gary, determined not to lose sight of Malvar. But at a left turn, the light caught red. Gary managed to rush through at the last moment. Bobby Woods was forced to slam on his brakes hard. He was helpless, watching the green truck disappear with Malvar.

Gary sped home.

Inside, Gary instructed Malvar to go through his cleaning routine. He had her use the washroom and wash up. After intercourse, Gary wrapped his arm around her neck. There he began strangling Malvar but determined she fought back, digging her fingernails into the skin of Gary's arm. "She fought back really hard. She fought the most of any of the ladies." She gouged his skin, and he screamed at her to stop.

"I'll let you go if you stop scratching me and rolling in the bed!" She didn't give up.

Infuriated, Gary grabbed a pair of pantyhose and tied them around her neck, choking Malvar to death. "Finally, she was just out of energy. I was just, like, thank God she was dead, and she wasn't fighting anymore."

Left with a torn, bleeding arm, Gary poured battery acid over the scratches and bandaged it. The acid burned away, marring his arm to the point the scratches left by Malvar were hidden. He dumped her body that night south of Kent-Des Moines Road and left her in a gully.

Bobby Woods hesitated to approach the police due to their professions, but finally, on May 3rd, he filed a missing person's report.

Several days later, her father and older brother stopped by. They told Bobby to get in the truck. They were going to drive around in search of Marie.

For four hours, the three men drove around the neighborhoods of South 216th Street. Their eyes scanned the driveway in hopes of finding a sign of their beloved Marie. In the afternoon, Bobby Woods recognized Gary's maroon pickup parked out the front of 216 Military Road.

It was the same truck that sped away with Marie inside.

The three parked the car and waited, watching the house for several hours. It appeared two men were inside; the identity of the second man has never been uncovered.

They called the police.

Two Des Moines detectives, one of whom was Bob Fox, knocked on Ridgway's front door that day, though they did not go inside. Gary answered their questions calmly. He admitted that he had a record for soliciting sex workers, but he claimed to have never picked up Marie Malvar. Bob Fox did not push the matter any further; he had known Gary a long time since the two worked together as teenagers at a local supermarket. Fox was inclined to believe Gary over Malvar's pimp. The file was tucked away, and the disappearance of Marie Malvar would be forgotten for some time.

Enough time for Gary to go on and kill many more.

The Second Summer

May 5th, a local family decided to go out and hunt for mushrooms together near Southeast 244th Street near Maple Valley. It was out in the country surrounded by thick trees far from the Strip. As they searched the ground for fungus, they stumbled upon a terrible surprise. A fully clothed body was lying in the cold earth with a brown paper bag pulled over her head. Like the rafter from the previous year, they'd thought it was a mannequin abandoned in the woods. But when they pushed back the paper with a long stick, they realized the horror before them was actually a dead body, who would later be identified as Carol Christensen.

Christensen was only twenty-one years old on May 3, 1983, when she worked as a waitress at the Barn Door Tavern. Her shift ended a half-hour after two, and she walked out the two doors, never to be seen again. At some point that night, she had been stopped by Gary and brought to his home, where he killed her. He dressed her body, leaving the bra inside out, then drove out to the Maple Valley dumpsite, leaving a dead trout across her throat and another atop her left breast. Raw ground beef was set inside her left palm, and a green wine bottle was positioned between her legs. Gary later would tell investigators the food was to draw wild animals to the body. According to Gary, there was no particular reason for the staging of the body, and the wine bottle meant nothing other than it was lying around his house.

The police identified Christensen quickly enough as her wallet contained her driver's license.

The winter air thawed away as the spring turned into summer. The heat drew in more women who turned to sex work for some extra cash. With only two bodies discovered in 1983, the initial fear dwindled away. Many of the women thought the killer had moved elsewhere. But they had never been more wrong. Gary was still on the move, and three more women were to meet a tragic fate.

The next to be killed was Martina Authorlee on May 22, 1983. Ridgway had spent the first part of his day attending a swap meet. As people passed by inspecting the items he was selling, they were clueless about the evil agenda for the evening. The following day he killed Cheryl Wims. Like Martina Authorlee, she was only eighteen years old.

May 31st, Gary stood in front of an atm Pacific Highway South at 11:44 p.m. He waited as the machine spit out $20 cash. Yvonne "Shelly" Antosh was last seen an hour later when she left the Ben Carol Motel. Ridgway "picked her up on Highway 99 … or uh, maybe uh, the Central District." They drove back to his home and had sex in his bedroom, where he used his hands first to strangle her, then a ligature.

Several days prior to the tragic death of Antosh, a custodian arrived at the Sea-Tac Airport. He went about their routine, running the vacuum back and forth over the carpet at Gate B4. He spotted the shiny plastic of a driver's license, forgotten on the floor. The custodian dutifully brought it to the lost and found. The information was reported to the police. It was revealed that the license belonged to a missing person; no officer arrived to pick it up, and the license was routinely destroyed. Valuable evidence such as fingerprints was lost due to negligence. The photo and name belonged to Marie Malvar. Gary drove to the airport after he killed Malvar and left her license on the floor to confuse the police.

It had been late spring when the beautiful, young Carrie Rois agreed to take a drive far away from the Strip with a trick. She rode all the way up to the summit of Snoqualmie Pass to watch the snowfall. She returned safely, albeit a bit intoxicated. Still, her friends noted the driver—a white male wearing a brown baseball cap, driving a truck that matched the description of Gary Ridgway's father's vehicle. And when her friends asked, she told them that he was "kind of weird." But that hadn't been the last of her weird encounters. Sometime in June, Rois vanished. She'd fallen victim to Ridgway's rage.

Gary's spree had hit the year mark. "And all the rage and the . . . some of 'em I took . . . took the towel and wrapped around their neck and pulled 'em and killed 'em. Some I used, uh, uh, a tie and a towel, and I pulled 'em back, and I put my legs in the back of her back on some of the women and just pulled as hard as I could to kill 'em. I, uh, I did it because I hated them. And I had . . . and after I killed 'em I mighta screwed a few of 'em, but I didn't give a shit. They were just pieces of trash to me. They were . . . they were garbage."

On June 8, 1983, he picked up and murdered twenty-year-old Constance Noan. He'd describe her as, "you know the *real* pretty one?" The day she disappeared, Noan phoned her boyfriend from the Red Lion Inn, telling him to expect her home in twenty minutes. She'd just met up with some friends to purchase cocaine. Instead of returning home, she ran into Ridgway at the Inn. He used his assuming demeanor to instill trust, and they agreed on a date. They talked about sex, and she mentioned the fifteen-year-old red Camaro she owned. She got in the truck and drove to a vacant lot just south of the airport. It was around six in the evening. Out of the truck, they walked about twenty feet and began having sex. He positioned himself behind her and reached to touch Noan's breasts, but she told him not to. It was enough of a trigger. Anger filled him, and after he climaxed, he strangled her.

With Noan's body lying on the still ground, Gary got up and removed the shovel from his truck. Metal tugged against the earth as he dug a shallow grave, rolling Noan in. He inserted stones into her vagina before piling dirt onto her and covering the site with sticks and brush to make it blend in. "I had to bury her because I had a tendency . . . not a tendency . . . of wanting to go back and screw them while they are dead. But I didn't do that. I had to bury her because I wouldn't go back."

He toyed with the idea of stealing her Camaro, but he decided against it, chucking the keys along the highway as he returned home, back to his everyday life.

A day afterward, Tammy Liles was picked up from the Strip by Gary and disappeared.

On June 18, 1985, Keli Kay McGinness fulfilled Gary's fantasy of a pretty blonde. "Blondes were special. And I think there were at least four or five blondes. I don't remember having sex after I killed them. I always liked blondes with big breasts. They were the high-priced hookers, and they were my special goal—to go out and get a blond lady and have sex with her and kill her. She was at the top of the list." He killed her that summer night, but they'd met previously. On February 23, 1983, Gary had dated the seventeen-year-old. They drove to a ballpark behind Sunset

Junior High School on South 140th Street, where their liaison was disturbed by a police patrol. He'd wait until that night in June to kill her.

July rolled around. The newspaper continued to print out stories about women who were potentially missing. It did little to deter the sex workers.

Kelly Ware was a cautious twenty-two-year-old who was nervous about working in the Sea-Tac area and instead hung around Chinatown and Aurora. Two weeks into July, she called her parents; it was the last time they heard from her. Ridgway went through his routine. He dumped her body at the South Airport site.

But after a few days, he returned.

It was late, and his son Matthew slept soundly in the truck. They'd just finished celebrating his son's birthday party, but that did little to deter Gary's evil desires. He had sex with Kelly Ware's corpse. As he finished returning to the truck, the sound of police sirens filled the lonely night. The Port of Seattle officers started asking Ridgway questions, wanting to know what he was up to. He explained he'd only stopped to use the restroom. They let him and his son go on their way.

A few days passed.

Gary returned to Ware. He had sex with her corpse one last time then dug a shallow grave to bury her. He stood back, admiring the way he hid her body so close to the road and out of sight. It would be the last time Gary would use the airport location for his dates.

Unlimited Supply of
Potential Victims

On the one-year anniversary of Wendy Coffield's death, a press conference was called to provide a summary of the Green River investigation. There was little news, except the police feared the number of murders could be double and worse, they believed the killer was still at work hunting the area. They'd looked into hundreds of suspects. There were still no solid leads. To the women working, Detective Richard Kaske directed his attention to them. "We've said it before, and we'll say it again: Don't get into cars with people you don't know. All signs point to a psychopathic personality who is preying on single women. All the prostitution out on the highway has given the killer a virtually unlimited supply of potential victims. These girls are just walking to their fate."

It was a fate twenty-two-year-old Tina Thompson would meet ten days later. That night in Ridgway's home, she struggled beneath him as he attempted to strangle her. She fought away from him, lunging to escape. But Gary caught her right at his front door. He struck her down and killed her. He drove her body to Highway 18 near 1-90, where he buried her beneath a layer of plastic.

Shortly after Gary added Thompson to one of his makeshift graveyards, a local man decided to pick apples. While he pulled fruit from the trees, he discovered the broken and fragmented remains of Shawnda Summers. Her body laid in a shallow grave beneath an apple tree and had been decomposing for almost a year. It was practically unidentifiable to investigators.

Gary walked along the road of Leisure Time Resort with his son Matthew. Tall trees reached up to the sky. The smell of bonfires lingered in the air. He'd visit here on vacations and weekend trips. There, seventeen-year-old April Buttram's corpse was left by Gary among a pile of young trees in late August. "I, um, talked my parents into buying a membership, uh, of the campground there because I could always go up and walk that road and, uh, knowing that there's a woman there." Leisure Time Resort became one of his favorite places to vacation.

It was a place to spend time with his son. And it was on Matthew's birthday, Ridgway strangled twenty-six-year-old Debbie May Abernathy. He was off work for the Labor Day weekend holiday.

On September 12th, Tracy Winston finished her last day in jail after serving for prostitution. Later that day, she picked up the phone and contacted a man whom she'd gone on dates with prior, a previous client of hers. She wanted to meet up and hoped he'd give her some rent money. He agreed, and after driving Winston to pay her rent, he dropped her off at Northgate Mall. A friend would later claim that they saw the nineteen-year-old three days later, but she never returned home the night of the 12th or contacted her family again.

She'd had a night with Gary Ridgway, and he brought her body to Cottonwood Park. A place where he brought previous girlfriends. "Like Cottonwood Park was a good place, along the river, and it was a while after the other ones were found, so that's why I chose it," he'd later explain. But perhaps, bringing Winston to a place with a history for Ridgway was, in fact, fulfilling fantasies he'd kept lingering in the depths of his mind.

Michigan native Kim Nelson had been a sex worker for several years, living in multiple cities along the west coast. With short bleached-blonde hair and long legs, Nelson was striking and nearly six feet tall. She'd moved to Seattle in August but had already been arrested several times. It was sometime that September when Nelson headed out near the Western Six Motel on the Strip to turn some trick.

She drove off with a client, who had an old tan Ford truck, to a dark and abandoned parking lot. He reached down and revealed a three-foot-long tire iron in his hand, telling Nelson he was going to kill her "just like I killed the rest of them. You bitches are all alike, nigger lovers." The tire iron flew down on her as the man whacked her over and over. Gripped with fear and the will to survive, Nelson reached for the door handle, but there wasn't one. As the onslaught continued, she managed to roll the window down and pull herself free from her attacker. She scrambled away, doing her best to memorize the license plate, but it was smeared with mud, and the numbers were hard to read.

The driver sped away.

On September 28th, Gary Ridgway clocked out of the paint shop at 3:20 in the afternoon. Several hours passed, then he picked up Maureen Feeney in Seattle, a kind woman who'd been working at a daycare and recently turned to prostitution to make extra cash. In the back of his truck, Gary killed her then drove back to Leisure Time Resort. He laid her body beside a barbed-wire fence. It was midnight, and Gary slinked back to his truck in the shield of darkness, stopping. A work crew passed by. Their lights broke his cover, but they did not stop. Gary would later return to have sex with Feeney's body beside the fence.

The humid heat of summer had turned into the cool air of fall. Detective Reichert continued pursuing his elusive killer. More and more reports of missing women arrived at the police department. Desperate for a lead, Reichert continued scouring through the woods, checking around the airport, and hoped to discover any clue, fearing to find another body.

But it wouldn't be long until another victim of the Green River Killer surfaced. Gary had not slowed down. He murdered Mary Sue Bello after leaving work on October 11, 1983, at 6:35 p.m.; he withdrew $40 at 7:51 p.m. The night of her murder, Gary drove to milepost 34 just off Highway 410. He parked his truck and dragged Bello's body through the forest. The thick line of trees masked his malevolence as he pulled the weight deeper into the forest with hopes to hide her away forever. When he was finished, he returned to his truck and drove away, chucking her sunflower dress and sandals out the window three miles from where her naked body rested.

Pammy Avent was murdered on October 26, 1983. She'd left her mother's that evening at 7:20 and was never seen again.

The day after Avent's death, a teenage couple explored several vacant lots south of the airport, searching for apples. The young woman caught sight of a snake. It slithered across stones. The woman raced over to catch it, but her foot caught, and she stumbled onto the dirt and sticks. She rose as the agitated dust floated around. Something peculiar stuck out of the earth. Horror gripped the young woman's heart. She'd fallen right over the skeletal remains of Constance Noan.

A group of Explorer Eagle Scouts was brought in by the police to help search the area for any jewelry or clothes. They combed through the vast vacant land while the medical examiners removed Noan's remains. They realized this victim had been buried, and a jagged stone was found in the center of her midsection. Clothes and jewelry were not found, but a scout located another skeleton fifty yards away from Noan, belonging to Kelly Ware. Her body was buried beneath overgrown foliage with debris and tin cans littered on top.

Four bodies had turned up in the same vicinity within the year. Homicide detectives knew they had to be connected, but the vacant lots with empty homes were vast with no witnesses near. And if their killer was burying the bodies, who knew how many were lying silent beneath the cold dirt. They were left with no other choice but to lead a massive search. Combing through the airport property would take time, close to a week, but it was vital. Investigators predicted this could be a copycat killer. There were too many differences between these bodies and those of the Green River murders.

At Kenworth, Gary was informed he'd be switching to the night shift on November 1st. The news infuriated him. The night was for Gary to drive down the streets and hire prostitutes. Daylight would make the chore of hiding bodies even more challenging. Filled with rage on the night of October 30th, Gary went out for a release.

Denise Plager promised to return home with a Halloween costume for her friend's child. At 3 p.m., she was dropped off at the bus station but never came back with the costume. It rained that Sunday night as Gary moved Plager's body near Exit 38. The autumn rain fell onto his shoulders and head as he left her body between two logs.

Unobtained Revenge

The tall Kim Nelson had ended up back in jail earlier that October. During her sentence, she told police about her encounter with the man in the old tan Ford truck who beat her with a tire iron. She promised the next time she saw the truck, she would grab that license plate. Nelson had been close friends with Denise Bush and told several people that if she ever ran into the Green River Killer, she'd make him regret his decisions.

Kim Nelson would have her chance encounter with the killer.

On October 30th, she walked out of jail and went straight back to work. On November 1st, she and her friend Paige Miley left the Ben-Carol Motel around 11 a.m. to pick up some johns in the morning. They sat on a nearby bus bench and waited. Miley landed one almost immediately; she said goodbye to Nelson and left, promising to be back within the hour. Now, it was time for Nelson to wait. She'd been out of jail for two days and needed the extra cash.

Cars sped by while she waited. Finally, one stopped. Even with her years of street smarts and passion to sniff out the killer, Gary fooled Nelson.

She unknowingly climbed into the truck of the Green River Killer. The same one she'd vowed to get revenge on.

Fifteen minutes passed, Paige Miley returned unsurprised to find Nelson wasn't there. She assumed she was with a client and would be back shortly.

But Nelson would never return that day—or the following.

Gary had driven Nelson to his home, where they made their way to the bedroom to have sex. If Gary had attacked Nelson earlier that September, she didn't make the connection then. He began strangling her. Nelson fought back, but it wasn't enough. She died the same way Denise Bush had. He removed her clothing and jewelry and wrapped her body in the carpet. It was daytime, and Gary had to move quickly. He flung her body into the truck bed after backing it up to the front door. Nelson was left beneath the trees at Exit 38.

"Where's your tall blonde friend?"

Underneath the same bus shelter, Paige Miley glanced up to see a man driving a red pickup truck. It'd only been about a day since Nelson disappeared. The man was interested in a car date, but Miley's sharp instincts kicked in.

Uneasiness settled over her. She and Nelson had only been together for a few short minutes yesterday, which meant this man had seen them together during that time. If Nelson had met the Green River Killer, Miley correctly assumed she was looking straight into his eyes. Gary pressed to go on a date, but Miley refused, and he drove off. But when Nelson was reported missing several days later, her friend contacted the police and provided a license plate number as well as an accurate physical description of Ridgway, but it would be several years before Miley's account would be used in the investigation.

November 13th, a light drizzle fell over the crew who hadn't stopped their search around the airport. The holidays were fast approaching, yet they couldn't risk slowing down. A search dog whined and whimpered. It did not provide any direction, only barked as the handler tried to lead the dog away. The handler called over the supervising police, and they began digging. Underneath the dreary sky, they unearthed the forgotten remains of Mary Meehan, who had been missing for over a year. Her body was removed to be identified.

"My God," the pathologist conducting the autopsy gasped. "...In the right lower quadrant of the abdomen, there are multiple fetal bone fragments. This appears to constitute a complete fetal skeleton." A moment of silence fell over everyone. This killer was more of a monster than man.

This monster was determined to keep playing games with the police. Gary returned to the remains of Kimi-Kai Pitsor and moved her skull. He knew if the skull was away from the body, then the task force would spend precious time searching around it. "They'll waste all kind of man hours thinking the rest of the body's in there," he later said.

That November, Detective Larry Gross, a member of Reichert's initial investigation team, came upon the name Gary Ridgway while investigating the death of Marie Malvar. He decided to meet with Ridgway for an interview. There was little reason to raise any alarm. The truck painter met with Gross and admitted to hiring sex workers, but he'd never had any contact with Marie Malvar. Gross left, doubtful someone like Gary was their killer. He didn't fit the Federal Bureau of

Investigation's psychological profile, nor was he anything like Ted Bundy.

It wasn't long until the skull's discovery on December 14, 1983. Winter air swirled around Mountainview Drive as a man walked along its shoulder. Much to his horror, his walk was interrupted by the discovery of Pitsor's skull. It sat upon a pile of leaves. No leaves were on top of it, suggesting it hadn't been there for long.

Letter Written

Gary's home needed a new roof that December. While the roofers replaced the shingles, Ridgway drove off to hire a sex worker. He hired one, drove to his home, hoping for privacy, but the workers were still present. Disappointed, he took his date to a parking lot near the Southcenter Mall. They climbed into the cramped back seat of his truck, and Gary killed her. He could not recall if nineteen-year-old Lisa Yates was the woman he killed that day, but she disappeared that December, and at some point, Gary placed Yates' body near Kim Nelson.

Dawn White walked along Pacific Highway South with another sex worker in later December or early January when Gary Ridgway began circling in his maroon truck. It was around 2 in the afternoon. He finally stopped and met them at Larry's Market. She and her friend got inside the pickup but were immediately put off. Ridgway came across as paranoid, telling the girls he'd been arrested twice by two vice decoys. He asked both girls to show their identifications and prove they weren't cops. Then he talked about dating them but didn't have enough cash for both, so he chose White over her friend. Her eyes flickered down to a roll of plastic, and she asked to see his id. He removed his license, and she read the name, Gary Ridgway.

After agreeing to a date, Gary said he had to leave for a short while and purchase something for this truck. He drove off, leaving White with her friend. While he was away, the police arrived at the market parking lot and told the girls to go.

Later that afternoon, White looked up Gary's phone number and called him, telling him the police showed up in the parking lot that day. They made plans to meet one another at Randy's Restaurant on East Marginal Way. White was sure to bring her friend and pimp along, slightly put off by Gary's behavior. At their second meeting, Gary told White about how he'd contracted syphilis and herpes previously. He wasn't interested in the date anymore. He strangely mentioned a girlfriend in Portland who went missing but had recently been found. She left Ridgway after an hour but had been so put off by his behavior she called police the following month to report her experience.

With the new tip, Detective Randy Mullinax went ahead and opened a new file on Gary. Mullinax pulled his history of soliciting an undercover cop and his recent interview with Detective Gross.

The months pressed forward, and the investigation ramped itself up. The Green River Task Force was reinforced and composed of two lieutenants, four sergeants, a dozen detectives, and twenty-two plainclothes street cops. "We were confident that the whole thing would be over in a few months. None of us believed it would take any longer than that. We all thought we'd have the guy in jail and that we'd all be back doing what we were supposed to be doing before anyone realized we were gone. Shit, were we wrong," a task force member recounted.

More were added to the suspect list, nearing a thousand names. To manage the immense list, three groups were created. A group: suspects in close proximity to the Strip with a record of violence. B group: those who were capable of violent crime but not linked to the Strip. C group: every other name received.

The list of potential victims was long and highly inaccurate. There were far more women missing than officially counted for, and the detectives were left with no choice but to sift through and find the names of those missing from previous prostitution arrests. Two detectives went to work, sifting through the list of arrests and figuring out who was genuinely missing and not on the run. The tedious job paid off when a potential witness came through—Kimi-Kai Pitsor's pimp.

After being assured he would not be arrested, Pitsor's pimp recounted the night in April 1983 when he last saw Kimi-Kai get into a green pickup truck with a white shell camper. He described the man with a pockmarked face and dark hair, in his twenties or thirties. It wasn't a perfect account, and the man Pitsor's pimp saw could have taken Kimi-Kai elsewhere before she was murdered, but the word was spread, and police were on the lookout for suspicious green trucks.

Mary West stepped out of her aunt's house on February 6, 1984, at 11:30 in the morning. The sixteen-year-old walked several blocks to Rainier Avenue, where she was picked up by Ridgway. He already had a spot that he figured would be "a good place to have a date and kill a woman" and took West to Seward Park.

Gary tucked a blanket underneath his arm, and in the cold, late winter, walked up a trail. They stopped after walking a bit in the woods. Gary laid the blanket down, and the two began to have sex. Then it was time for Ridgway to strike. He distracted West, suggesting that a car was driving toward them. She lifted her head, and that was all he needed to strangle her. West's hands reached, tugging at Gary, thrashing as her nails dug into his back.

"If you stop fighting, I'll let you go," Gary lied.

But the struggle between the two of them continued until West had no fight left, and she was overpowered. Breathing hard, Gary began his usual process, dragging West's limp body deeper into the woods, where he covered debris and dirt over her.

Finished, he returned to his truck. It was a weekday, and he had work later.

On Valentine's Day, Denise Plager's remains were found by a man looking for moss near a state park. On March 13th, a soldier in a convoy stopped at Exit 38 and discovered Lisa Yates' body between two logs.

At the end of February 1984, a letter arrived at the *Seattle Times* postal box address to the *Post-Intelligencer.* "Very important" was written on the envelope. Inside was a typed letter from Gary himself, sent in a desperate hope to lead investigators astray. It was forty numbered lines with words running into one another and no spaces.

With spaces added, the letter reads as follows: what you eed to no about the green river man dont throw away

1) first one boken or on dislocate arm why

2) one black in river had a stone in the vagina why

3) why some in river some above ground some underground

4) insurance who got it

5) whos to gain by there deaths

6) truck is out of state father had painted or in river

7) some had fingernals cut off

8) he had sex after they dead he smokes

9) he chews gum

10) chance first one blackmaled him

11) you work me or no body

12) think changed his mo bussnessman or sellman

13) car and motel reservation

14) man seen big lugage out of motel was heavy needed help

Keys id card at road i8 whos

15) wheres close some rings and misc

16) out of state cop

17) dont kill in our area lookin outside

18) one had old scarse

19) mo maple had red wine lombrosc some fish and dumped there

20) any drugs or selling

21) head found who found it where is rest

22) when did they died day or night

23) what burn there mouths or is it a trick

24) why take some cloths and leave rest

25) the killer wheres at least one ring

26) realest man is one man

27) long haul truck driver last seen with one

28) some had rope markes on neck and hands

29) one bla e in river had bra on only

30) all strangled but with defer metheds

31) one black in river and worked for metro

32) most had pimps betting them

33) escort modeling forced them off fear of deth

34) maybe pimp hater get back at them

34) who finds the bones what are they there for

35) man whith gun or knife

36) some one paid to kill one others aret hide it

37) kill who they are or is it what they are

38) any dead difer then restt

39) it could a man portlad some worked there

40) what kind of man is this

there was a book lift at dennys i got this ot of it bilongs to cop call me fred

With acts of necrophilia, missing fingernails, and the stones inserted in the vagina, it was clear this letter contained evidence kept hidden from the public. A number of the claims made in Gary's letter were facts, such as line 19, clearly referring to the red wine Lambrusco found with the pregnant Carol Christensen. But in an attempt to hopefully throw the police from his trail, Gary sprinkled in lies, such that the killer was a smoker who chewed gum and worked as a long-haul truck driver.

The FBI quickly wrote the letter off as a prank and thought it was someone within the police who had access to the intel. Gary would admit to writing the letter years later.

The Final Few

Cindy Smith wanted to leave California and come back home to Seattle. When she called her mom about moving home, an airline ticket was paid for, and Cindy was on her way back. She landed on March 13th, spending her first few hours back home with her parents. She walked out the front door around 11 a.m. intending to visit her sister or apply to be a topless dancer near the Strip.

But unfortunately for Smith, Gary's shift didn't start until 4 p.m. And after he murdered Smith, he left her body close to the road, beside Green River Community College campus. He worried about drivers seeing her body, so he used the surrounding garbage, including a heavy piece of wood, to conceal her.

A week later, at a Little League field, a dog ran up to its owner holding a human leg bone within its jaw. It was the same field several people had made complaints about a foul smell earlier that year. Even Detective Reichert went to investigate the stench, but nothing had been found until now. The leg bone belonged to fourteen-year-old Wendy Stephens. At some point in 1983, fourteen-year-old Wendy Stephens ran away from her home in Denver, Colorado, and made it all the way to Seattle. It was during the day when Gary took her life. He wanted to ensure she was dead since his last attempt at murder had failed, and the woman escaped him. She was his youngest victim and would remain unidentified until September 2020.

The day after Stephens' skeleton was found, the entire field was searched. Within one hour, a second body was uncovered.

More skeletons were unearthed as the winter turned into spring. Debbie Abernathy's remains were discovered by an elk hunter walking through the roads on March 31st. While far away near Star Lake, another man hunting for mushrooms found Delores Williams on the same day. Clusters of bodies were showing up, and detectives began plotting a map. They realized Gary had several sites he used, all connected by secondary state highways. These sites contained around five bodies within the same area, like the initial victims pulled from the river. As the bodies had been discovered early on, Gary had known to move them. He left them buried beneath debris and garbage as if to send a message—those he killed were nothing more than trash.

And on April 1, 1984, Star Lake became a focus. Six women in total would be discovered over several years there. It was a place Ridgway said, "where I could put a woman … a bunch of women…. It was, hey, fantastic…. It was, uh, woodsy, secluded, and, uh, it was a, a, site that I figured nobody would find her at, and uh, if they did, it would be a couple years later. Wouldn't be anything, you know, no, noth-nothing left of her…. I could go down there during the day and have sex with her. Nobody see me from, from the top. There was a road on the top and there's a road on the bottom. They couldn't see me. And even if it did, a car come by, I could lay down." It was a location Gary knew well, and had even spent hot summer days swimming in the cool lake waters with family.

The intensive search to cover the entire area began on the morning of the 1st. Light rain fell from the sky as the team worked, scouring the area bit by bit. Yellow crime scene tape fluttered in the breeze. It only took the team two hours until two more bodies were added to the count. They belonged to Sandra Gabbert and Terry Milligan.

A professional tracker was brought in, looking over one of Gary's makeshift graves and peered at the loose dirt, finding the faintest shoe print.

"The tracks were obviously made when the person could see quite well, probably during daylight. The person could see the trail to carry the body to the location, find the brush and cover the body. Signs give no indication as to the predetermination of depositing the body by the log, however, there is a sign of only one person ... He didn't just throw the body into the brush, but attempted to cover it with leaves, ferns, loose debris." Gary's shoe print was the one real piece of Gary they'd found.

The following day, Alma Smith was found in the woods along Star Lake Road.

Murderous Rampage Slows

In the early months of 1984, the murders began to taper off, and Gary's initial wave of violence and destruction slowed.

The use of the clusters revealed a specific pattern. Gary tested a new site with one victim. If time passed and no one discovered the body, he knew it was safe to add to it, dumping many more within a short period, and once one was found, he'd never return. But between the dry land and river cases, there were some differences, leading investigators to wonder if they were created by the hands of two different killers.

After his name was brought up several times within the investigation, he willingly arrived at the Green River Task Force headquarters to meet with Randy Mullinax to be interviewed. He sat across from Mullinax and admitted to having dated several of the missing women. He even admitted to speaking with Kim Nelson's friend, Paige Miley.

Mullinax listened to the average-looking man whose small eyes moved behind thick round glasses. Nothing made Ridgway stand out from the others on the long suspect list, but Mullinax decided to arrange a lie detector test for the next month.

May 7, 1984, Gary Ridgway sat down to take a lie detector test, and the polygraph examiner decided Gary was not lying. Mullinax, like Detective Gross, decided there was little cause to investigate Gary any further.

Still, more bodies were being unearthed. In late May, two children were enjoying the warm spring air and building a fort outside when they found another body.

Rebecca Garde came forward in November 1984 with her story about the man who choked her while they were out in the forest and her narrow escape from death. She identified Gary Ridgway, and once again, his name rose to the top of the list of potential suspects.

December 1984, Theodore Robert Bundy had read the news and was intrigued by the Green River Murders occurring in his home state of Washington. He penned a letter to Robert Keppel offering to provide advice and insight into a killer's mind. Keppel agreed to fly down and sit across from America's most notorious serial killer.

The primary advice provided by Bundy was that police keep the victim sites under constant surveillance. He described the strong connection a killer has with where they leave the bodies. It was almost a guarantee the killer would return and relive the events. And while Gary did return to his sites, he stayed away once the police found one body. For Bundy, it was an opportunity to bargain with the police and gain more time. Though his advice had some validity, he offered little in discovering the true identity of the Green River Killer.

Through the fall and winter, the task force continued their search, scraping away at the collection of evidence and information they'd amassed. Two new skeletons discovered were added to the growing list. Pedestrians stumbled upon them while out in the woods, and the task force worked tirelessly to give the bodies a name and face, pouring through possible victim lists.

But the killing appeared to have come to a sudden stop in 1984. Police thought their killer had died, was in prison for other charges, or had become discouraged with all the police "decoys" set along the Strip.

At first, Gary insisted to his lawyers the last murder was in 1985. "The last one was in 1985. I went to Tacoma to get some new tires. I saw this lady I'd dated before. She lived in Des Moines. She needed a ride back to her apartment. I think . . . I'm quite certain . . . I killed her in my truck, somewhere in Federal Way. I took her body out to Highway 410. I remember, because the canopy flew off my truck on Highway 18 on the way home." This was either a lie or a sign that Gary's memory was failing him. He'd kill several times, though at a much slower rate.

"None of the so-called experts believe a serial killer will ever stop. But you did. And that's great. But . . . how did you stop?" Michele Shaw, one of Gary's lawyers, would later ask. Tears formed in the corner of his eyes.

"I met Judith." He became emotional, and his words choked. "I met Judith," he repeated once more.

Judith Lorraine

February 1985, forty-year-old Judith Lorraine had finally left a dysfunctional nineteen-year-long marriage. She'd moved into a small, cheap apartment near Seattle with a roommate. Close by was White Shutters, a country-styled tavern hosting weekend dances.

Judith had heard about an organization called Parents Without Partners that held socials on the weekend at the White Shutters Tavern. She decided to enjoy a night as a newly single mother and attend one of the events with a friend.

They ordered beers and sat at a table talking, enjoying the music. It was one of the first times Judith was enjoying her new lease on life. Two men walked over and struck up a conversation, asking if the women would like to dance. One caught Judith's attention. He wore slim-fit jeans, a western-style shirt, cowboy boots and presented himself as wholesome and proper.

He introduced himself as Gary Ridgway. He was out celebrating his birthday, which had been on the 18th.

"Happy Birthday," she said, then asked about his age. Gary told her thirty-six years old. Immediately, Judith assumed she was too old for Gary. But the two began dancing through the night until the bar closed. He didn't seem to mind the four-year age gap, and he and his buddy invited the two women out to grab breakfast. It was several hours after midnight. In the back seat of the van, Judith cozied up beside Gary. They laughed as the sharp turns gave them an excuse to lean against one another, and when the car came to a stop, to Judith's surprise, the thirty-six-year-old planted a quick kiss right on her lips.

She immediately caught feelings.

At a friend's house, the night carried on. And before Judith knew it, she was cuddled up beside Gary alone in the living room. They shared intimate details about their lives. She learned about his previous marriages and his son, Matthew, whom he loved dearly. Soft kisses turned more passionate.

He asked if it was alright to kiss her that way, always sure to put her comfort first.

She told him it was all fine. And when the night came to an end, and the two men returned Judith and her friend to their cars at the White Shutters, Gary asked for Judith's phone number, and she eagerly recited it to him along with her address. She doubted he'd call her, but part of her desperately hoped he would.

How unaware she was of the man she'd kissed with a naive hope for more. The same hands that held her face had killed at least forty-nine women and left their lifeless bodies along the riverbank.

Two days went by. On February 23rd, Gary was brought in by the Green River Task Force and asked about Rebecca Garde. He admitted to choking her. At first, he claimed he did not know any of the victims, but he admitted to dating several after being shown several photos. He was sent home.

Judith excitedly told her roommate that the nice, polite guy had phoned her. Gary had called her back after his meeting with the task force. Perhaps he felt impervious or uncatchable. He'd met with the officers several times, passed a polygraph test, and went home every time.

An interview with the police wouldn't stop him from enjoying his life.

Judith got ready for her date with haste, putting on makeup and dressing up. She stood in awe of the handsome, clean-shaven man who arrived at her front door. She climbed into his pickup truck, the same one countless women had been strangled in and went out to dinner at a local diner. Conversing with Gary was easy for Judith. He wasn't condescending, and after that night, the weekly dates continued. They met at McDonald's and held hands under the table when no one looked. They giggled like silly children, completely smitten with one another. And after a month of regular dates and calls, Gary eventually invited Judith over to his Sea-Tac rambler.

Immediately, she noticed the carpet missing. Carpet used to haul a body to his truck in the middle of the day. Without missing a beat, he explained he had rented a bedroom to a couple with a young child, who was peeing on the floor. There was a horrible scent, so he had most of it ripped out. He gave her a home tour, showing off a room with a twin bed and toys strewn about. He explained it was his son's for when he came to visit. He'd shown his victims that room to help ease their minds before murdering them.

Eventually, they arrived at the bedroom, where Gary invited Judith to get into bed with him. "You know, Judith, it's probably about time we make love." Eagerly, Judith began to undress, but Gary stopped her, insisting that they wash first. It was a habit that they carried through the rest of their relationship. In Judith's mind, Gary was concerned with cleanliness during sex. Gary was a tender lover, always gentle and polite, putting her needs over his own. It was a stark contrast to the violent sex he paid for. In reality, Gary feared transmitting STDs. He'd never stopped his habit of hiring sex workers.

In March that year, a seventeen-year-old boy walked through the woods and found the remains of Carrie Rois, buried partly in the mud. Several days later, the investigators announced that the homicides had appeared to have stopped, though the search for the victims remained. The task force had almost twenty thousand tips of information called in.

Gary invited Judith to stay in his home in May and had a key made for her to spend the night if she liked.

She moved herself in, cleaning and doing his laundry, and when midnight came, she'd hop into bed and wait for Gary to come home. He walked through the front door at the same time every single night. "Hi there, what's new?" he always asked, without fail. He'd arrive covered in paint overspray from the factory, then showered, asking if she had as well. They had sex almost every single night unless he worked overtime. He'd tell her his allergies were terrible, or he was too exhausted.

And while Judith was being swept away in a whirlwind of a romance on June 11, 1985, a bulldozer operator tore through bushes in preparation for a tree farm. Sticking out of the dirt was a partial skull. It belonged to Denise Bush. Soon Judith met his family, including his mother, Mary Rita, who still held dominion over the family. They spent many weekends and holidays with Gary's parents. They went on trips with ten-year-old Matthew and introduced Gary to her children.

They lived a full schedule with plans almost every weekend. They visited the zoo with Matthew or headed off to the park, bringing along one of Judith's grandchildren. They took ferry boat rides, had picnics, and went to monster truck shows. Together they bought a brand-new camper to take on trips. Every once in a while, Gary would surprise Judith with splurging on a purchase. He purchased dirt bikes for camping trips, went out to Vegas, and even brought her and Matthew down to Disneyland.

"We were together all the time after that. I didn't have the desire to kill anymore. I didn't want to get caught, you know," Gary described.

Closer to the Killer

Ridgway's case was turned over to the FBI after Detective McAllister's investigation of the Rebecca Garde Guay incident was reviewed.

March 17, 1986, Gary willingly arrived at the task force headquarters to be questioned about his connection to Rebecca Garde Guay and their incident in the forest. He explained she'd bitten him enough to draw blood, and he only began choking her in self-defense, but he never slapped her. After being shown several photographs of the victims, he admitted to dating several of them. Gary claimed to have stopped hiring sex workers because of the murders, telling them the only time he assaulted one was Rebecca Garde. He told them about contracting venereal disease fifteen times and his compulsion to hire prostitutes.

People began calling him "Green River Gary" behind his back at work. The news of his police interviews was common knowledge, but none thought much more past it. It was only a joke. To his neighbors, Gary was described as a "nice guy" who spent time outdoors, gathered wood for his fireplace, walked Judith's poodle Peaches, and kept to himself.

In the summer of '86, three new victims had been discovered. The list of known dead had reached thirty-six.

In August of 1986, the friend of Kim Nelson was finally located in Las Vegas as a potential witness. Paige Miley sat down with police and was able to pull out a photograph of Gary Ridgway from a photo array and let the investigators know she gave Detective Reichert's original task force the man's license plate back in 1983 but had never heard back. They had lost the license plate number.

Gary returned to the top of the suspect list, and his case was reopened. Detectives found his second wife, Marcia. On September 14, 1986, she rode in the car, pointing out areas her ex-husband took her. Many were locations where victims had been discovered. And when previous case files were dug up, multiple witnesses had seen a victim climb into a vehicle that matched Gary's pickup at the time.

While the task force gathered more evidence on their new top suspect, Gary's rage would continue boiling over.

Burnette Patricia Barczak vanished off the streets on October 17, 1986. The nineteen-year-old had been living at the Airporter Motel on Pacific Highway South. Gary had just started working the swing shift at Kenworth when he murdered her.

After meeting with Gary's second wife, the trends were impossible for the task force to ignore. He'd been arrested in 1982 for hiring a police decoy; sex worker, Rebecca Garde, accused him of choking her. Police records showed they'd encountered Gary near the Little League field in 1982, yards from the burial site of several bodies. Even more shocking, three victims were connected to him. Eyewitnesses had seen pickup trucks matching Ridgway's during many of the victims' disappearances. He lived and worked nearby the Strip. It was a viable lead.

Investigators obtained a warrant.

Probably the Wrong Guy

On April 8, 1987, Judith was at the daycare she worked at when she heard men speaking at the front entrance. She was shocked to learn they'd arrived for her. They told her that they needed to talk. Confused and a bit scared, Judith sat in the car and was asked a series of questions. More shock set in as their house was to be searched. Gary was stopped after work. Hair and saliva samples were taken. His truck and vehicles were towed away. Carpet samples were cut from his home.

But a few weeks after the initial search of Ridgway's home and vehicles, it appeared the task force had the wrong man. The collected evidence could not be matched to anything obtained from the victims. The investigation into Gary was dropped, and once again, the task force was losing its momentum.

At home, Gary explained to a concerned Judith that the police sometimes made mistakes and picked up "the wrong guy." He said they'd probably grabbed about forty other guys. But none of that mattered. He was home now, and that must mean he was innocent. He and Judith went to work, putting their home back together after the police ran through it.

May 1988, construction workers digging post holes in Federal Way came upon the body of Debra Estes. The parents' tired search for their lost daughter had come to an end.

While the Estes family mourned the loss of "Muffin," close friends and family of the Ridgways opened their mailboxes to find wedding invitations. "To love and to cherish from this day forward…" Gary and Judith were married on June 12, 1988. They celebrated with a potluck in the same yard they had the wedding in. They danced and fed one another cake with plans to head to their honeymoon six days later. They drove to Oregon, and their first stop was Leisure Time Resort.

At Gary's suggestion, Judith quit her full-time job and stayed at home. She even took over managing the checkbook. Gary brought home paychecks and handed them straight to his wife. She watched the savings and made deposits, matching her husband's frugal habits. They purchased all their clothes, including underwear, second-hand. He didn't overeat and stayed trim, choosing simple meals like meat and potatoes with the occasional vegetable, and there was never any dessert. He allowed the rare treat of popcorn in the evening. Rarely did they eat out, except when there were coupons or a special discount.

On one occasion, supper got burned, so the couple decided to go out for hamburgers. Judith sat beside Gary in the truck. Her eyes followed the passing buildings when a sudden thought came to her. She asked Gary what a prostitute looked like. He pointed out the window over the steering wheel to a woman in high heels and fishnets. Judith was shocked to see a sex worker in broad daylight. She never knew why the question came to her mind.

During their second year of married life, they sold the rambler and purchased a new home. Gary continued with his perfect attendance at work, and they continued enjoying their days together. Some nights, Gary curled up with his wife on the sofa to watch a movie, but Judith noticed something about her husband. During violent physical scenes, Gary began to shift in his seat like he was extremely uncomfortable. At times, she looked to see Gary crying, or he'd leave to get water. If she asked, he acted as though everything was fine. She assumed it was post-traumatic stress disorder from serving in the Navy and learned it was best to leave him be.

October 11, 1989, the forty-ninth body looked up from a shallow grave. Another one pulled from the vacant lot near the golf course and close to the airport. The Green River Task Force had lost most of its momentum. Investigators were clueless as to how many were scattered throughout King County.

During an interview after his arrest, Gary Ridgway was shown a photo of a murdered woman named Marta Reeves. She disappeared in 1990, and her body was found at one of Ridgway's clusters. Upon speaking with investigators about dumping a victim at Highway 410, he said, "OK, then I killed her then, yeah. I, I agree, I killed a woman there, yes. But I thought it was in '87, '87 or '88 . . . I, I admit getting a, killing a woman there."

The years passed by, filled with busy camping trips, swap meets and spending time with family. They'd fallen into a happy rhythm of married life. They replaced the camper with a new motorhome and upgraded Gary's truck. In 1997, they bought their dream retirement home close to Lake Geneva in Auburn. Gary worked beside Judith, maintaining the yard and garden. They raised poodles together, whom they adoringly nicknamed their "children."

"I had much more to lose. I had a house, a family, and everything, and I didn't have no reason to go back. Sure, I've had problems, but I had Judith as an anchor to watch me, still. I still had problems with prostitution, but that's . . . going back and killing, it wouldn't help me."

The Final Kill

August 4, 1998, at 1:30 p.m., the owner of "All City Wrecking" locked up his office and headed home. He would return two days later and find the body of Patricia Yellowrobe positioned right outside the fence of the tow yard, fully clothed. Sometime after the owner left that Tuesday, Gary Ridgway arrived in his truck with an intoxicated Yellowrobe. They had sex in the back of his truck, but he became enraged by the fact she was "just layin' around." Yellowrobe wouldn't let Gary position himself behind her to have sex. "She didn't want to spend an extra three or four minutes to, to, uh, have me climax and be, have a customer. She just uh, said, 'You're over with,' you know, some'n like that, and, uh, got dressed and when we got out I was still angry at her, and ch-choked her." Mad, Gary wrapped his hands around Yellowrobe's neck, and he strangled her to death. Due to her level of intoxication, her body might have lacked any ability to withstand seconds of asphyxia. The autopsy revealed her death was caused by an overdose, and it would be several years until Gary admitted to taking her life.

After Yellowrobe's murder, panic consumed Gary. Unsure what to do, he left her body there beside the fence and drove away.

The Green River Task Force had been diminished to one single detective—Tom Jensen. Dave Reichert had risen through the ranks and had become the new sheriff. Other members moved on to new cases and with their lives. The landscape of the Strip had transformed. The seedy dancing taverns were torn down. Sex workers stopped hanging by the convenience stores and parking lots.

Years ticked by, and Jensen submitted DNA found among the victims to be tested every so often. It wasn't until the late 90s, technological advancement in DNA made a massive leap. Tiny fragments of a DNA strand showed repeating molecules that were unique in every human. Even old DNA could be resurrected and compared to collected samples. The process was called "short tandem repeats."

In October 2001, Jensen sent away the DNA records from the Green River killings for STR testing. They ran samples collected from Opal Mills, Marcia Chapman, and Carol Christensen. A perfect match had been found. It was the average, unassuming truck painter. Gary Leon Ridgway.

Police worked quickly, gathering evidence to obtain a search warrant. They wanted to have no doubts this was their killer, and they knew it would take several months to prepare a solid case for the prosecutor.

But Gary would drive straight to them.

On November 16th, Gary Ridgway drove up to a police decoy on Pacific Highway South, waving money through the car window. He mentioned the police might be watching him, so they agreed to meet at an ATM at a local bank's parking lot. The decoy gave the single. The vice squad was ready and arrested Gary as he drove to the meeting location.

He was found with $30 and latex gloves in his possession. He was charged and arrested for loitering. They released him, and Gary phoned his wife, asking if she'd pick him up. He walked out of Kent Jail to meet her at a K-Mart.

He told Judith he was stopped because he forgot to put his tailgate up. He'd only pulled over when the cop brought him in for questioning. "Probably thought I was someone else." She had no reason to doubt her husband. How could Judith even begin to understand what her husband was and what he was capable of? They enjoyed their Thanksgiving together with friends.

On November 30, 2001, the police finally arrested Gary Ridgway for the murder of Carol Christensen, Marcia Chapman, Opal Mills, and Cynthia Hinds. They arrived at the Kenworth factory at 11 a.m. to place him in handcuffs.

"Gary, we're detectives from the King County Sheriff's Office, and you are under arrest for the murder of several women in King County."

"Okay." It was all Gary said as he handed his lunchbox to an officer and climbed into the car.

His coworkers stopped, watching in horror and shock. The man they'd worked beside for so many years was a killer. Gary was left in a state of shock, and he was a little mad, "because I was tryin' to forget the Green River murders." As they drove to the Regional Justice Center, he was passive, only asking what would happen to his truck.

The Green River Killer

Over the next several days, many boxes were carried away from Ridgway's past and current homes, vehicles, motorhome, and safety deposit box. All stuffed with potential evidence to be compared with the backlog of evidence gathered over the past twenty years. Crime scene technicians peeled away at the carpet pads to the bare floor inside Gary's old house. There was no sign of the violent murders that occurred within the walls. In the Des Moines and Auburn homes, the houses were searched for bloodstains, clothing, or any type of trophy he would have kept stashed away. There was nothing. Spare bedrooms were stuffed to the brim with random items most likely meant to be sold off at swap meets. One of the searchers noted, "They were major pack rats, though. There was too much of everything in that split-level house, but it was clean, dusted, and reasonably neat in the living room and kitchen area."

While Judith was put up in a hotel room, Ridgway was locked away in an "ultra-security" cell in King County Jail. He would never come home to his wife again. He was denied bail. December 5, 2001, Gary Ridgway was formally charged with four counts of murder for Marcia Chapman, Opal Mills, Cynthia Hinds, and Carol Ann Christensen. He pleaded "not guilty."

On March 27, 2002, Gary Ridgway was charged with three more counts of aggravated murder. The coveralls pulled from his Kenworth locker had tiny dots of paint. Microscopic flecks of paint were found on several victims.

For the next six months, the Green River Task Force came up with a plan to understand Ridgway's motives and learn where he'd left the remaining victims. He was placed inside the office of the Green River Task Force. He slept on a mattress in a closely guarded room. There he underwent long hours of questioning and interviews. He went with investigators, locked up in handcuffs, through the woods, revealing where he'd left the bodies. He told the investigators he'd worn gloves and switched the shoes he wore, replaced the tires of his truck, and kept newspaper articles about the task force. But most shocking of all was that Gary believed the number of women murdered by his hands was upward in the seventies. He would later retract the story of there ever being an accomplice.

The biggest issue was handling Gary's faulty memory. He stumbled over his words as he did his best recollecting twenty years into the past. His information was mixed with lies, useless facts, and reports he read in the media. He told the investigators he'd hired six or seven hundred women over his lifetime and couldn't recall which ones he had murdered.

Eventually, they got to the bottom of why. Gary finally admitted he killed these women only because he wanted to. He no longer needed the rage or anger. His hatred for women became second to the will to murder. Taking the lives of women became more important than the sex itself. He told them about his acts of necrophilia, and after he returned to use their bodies, he bathed himself in a mixture of rubbing alcohol and Aqua Velva aftershave to kill germs and hide the odor.

He talked about the horrible fantasies he dreamed of in his mind. Gary described how he wanted to drive a massive pole through the women. "It was the arousal of watching, if I did it, it was the arousal of watching her in pain, dying. You live by . . . having guys put dicks in you, now you have a pole up you and you're gonna die that way. But I didn't do it. I thought about it. That would have been the ultimate if I was that crazy."

To hide the dark side of his life, he developed a series of codes. Phone numbers were jotted down to look like paint colors for Kenworth. He jotted down notes about landmarks where certain girls hung out and was sure to cross off the ones he'd murdered. It was hidden among grocery and to-do lists, written down on receipts. After killing a woman, he'd contact their pimp about meeting a second time or beg for a date, waiting at the agreed location.

As Gary lived among the investigators and spent hours discussing his life, his defense team worked out a plea bargain. He was to plead guilty to forty-eight counts of murder on November 5, 2003. He signed away his rights to a trial in exchange for avoiding the death penalty. His statement was read aloud to the courtroom by prosecutor Jeff Baird.

The Judge has asked me to state what I did in my own words that makes me guilty of these crimes. This is my statement:

I killed the forty-eight women listed in the State's second amended information. In most cases, when I murdered these women, I did not know their names. Most of the time, I killed them the first time I met them and I do not have a good memory for their faces. I killed so many women I have a hard time keeping them straight.

I have reviewed information and discovery about each of the murders with my attorneys, and I am positive that I killed each one of the women charged in the Second Amended Information.

I killed them all in King County. I killed most of them in my house near Military Road, and I killed a lot of them in my truck, not far from where I picked them up. I killed some of them outside. I remember leaving each woman's body in the place where she was found. I have discussed with my attorneys the "common scheme or plan" aggravating circumstance charged in all these murders. I agree that each of the murders I committed was part of a "common scheme or plan." The plan was: I wanted to kill as many women I thought were prostitutes as I possibly could. I picked prostitutes as my victims because I hate most prostitutes and I did not want to pay them for sex. I also picked prostitutes as victims because they were easy to pick up without being noticed. I knew they would not be reported missing right away, and might never be reported missing. I picked prostitutes because I thought I could kill as many of them as I wanted without getting caught.

Another part of my plan was where I put the bodies of these women. Most of the time I took the women's jewelry and their clothes to get rid of any evidence and make them harder to identify. I placed most of the bodies in groups, which I call "clusters." I did this because I wanted to keep track of all the women I killed. I liked to drive by the "clusters" around the county and think about the women I placed there. I usually used a landmark to remember a "cluster" and the women I placed there. Sometimes I killed and dumped a woman, intending to start a new "cluster," and never returned because I thought I might get caught putting more women there.

As each of the forty-eight names was read, Gary's voice answered back, "Guilty."

On December 18, 2003, King County Superior Court Judge Richard Jones looked Gary square in the eyes. He hoped the women he killed would return and haunt him in his dreams while he sits in prison. "As you spend the balance of your life in that tiny cell, surrounded only by your thoughts, please know the women you killed were not throwaways—pieces of candy in a dish placed upon this planet for the sole purpose of satisfying the murderer's desires." He was sentenced to forty-eight life terms.

It was the end of a terrible nightmare that had hung over King County.

It had taken twenty years.

He'd walked in the sunlight as a boring non-threatening man. A father and avid outdoorsman, who rummaged through swap meets and became the budding joke of his coworkers. He hid behind the facade of banality for more than twenty years, hiding the rage he festered for his ex-wives, girlfriends, coworkers, and mother. None knew the skilled killer beside them, who killed for the enjoyment of it.

To this day, Gary sits within his jail cell at the Washington State Penitentiary in Walla Walla. Some names and bodies of his victims remain lost to this day. They are waiting to be unearthed and remembered as those innocent lives fallen victim to Gary Leon Ridgway.

Bibliography

CNN, Cable News Network,
transcripts.cnn.com/show/ijvm/date/2014-01-10/segment/01.

Keppel, Robert D., and William Birnes. *The Riverman: Ted Bundy and I Hunt for the Green River Killer.* Pocket Books, 2010.

Mccarthy/Seattle, Terry. "River of Death." *Time*, Time Inc., 3 June 2002,
content.time.com/time/subscriber/article/0,33009,1002555-2,00.html.

"Murder Made Me Famous: The Green River Killer."

Prothero, Mark, and With Carlton Smith. *Defending Gary: Unraveling the Mind of the Green River Killer.* John Wiley & Sons, 2007.

Reichert, David. *Chasing the DEVIL: My TWENTY-YEAR Quest to Capture the Green River Killer.* St Martin's Paperbacks, 2006.

Rule, Ann. *Green River, Running RED: The Real Story of the Green River Killer—America's DEADLIEST Serial Murderer.* Gallery Books, 2019.

Seattle Times (various articles), 1993-2021.

Smith, Carlton, and Tomas Guillen. *The Search for the Green River Killer.* Signet True Crime, 2004.

Wood, Pennie. *She Married the Green River Serial Killer: The Story of an Unsuspecting Housewife.* Knotted Road Press, 2021.

www.ingramcontent.com/pod-product-compliance
Lightning Source LLC
Chambersburg PA
CBHW071913120726
48001CB00005B/1732